the salt book

the salt book

your guide to salting wisely and well, with recipes

Fritz Gubler and David Glynn
with Dr Russell Keast

APPLE

First published in the UK in 2013 by
Apple Press
7 Greenland Street
London NW1 0ND
United Kingdom
www.apple-press.com
 ISBN 978 1 84543 492 2

© Arbon Publishing, 2010

Arbon Publishing Pty Ltd
45 Hume St, Crows Nest NSW 2065, Australia
PO Box 623, Crows Nest NSW 1585
Telephone: +61 2 9437 0438
Facsimile: +61 2 9437 0288
Email: admin@arbonpublishing.com
or visit www.arbonpublishing.com

Managing Director: Fritz Gubler
Publisher: Carolen Barripp
Managing Editor: Raewyn Glynn
Communications Manager: Helen Cameron
Book Design: Stephen Smedley, Tonto Design
Photographer: Scott Cameron
Styling: Jane Collins

Contributors:
Dr Russell Keast: Senior Lecturer, Exercise and Nutrition Science, Deakin University, Australia
Farzan Contractor: Executive Chef, The Meat & Wine Co., Sydney, Australia
Stephane Jégat: Executive Chef, Kobe Jones Restaurant, Sydney, Australia
Jason Palmero: Executive Sous Chef, Kobe Jones, Sydney, Australia
Jude Messenger: Executive Chef, Plateau Restaurant, Taupo, New Zealand

Printed and bound by 1010 Printing Limited (China)

The ability to salt food properly is the single most important skill in cooking.

THOMAS KELLER, THE FRENCH LAUNDRY COOKBOOK

Contents

Introduction   8

Salt Wise
Know Your Salt   14
Tasting Salt   22
Too Much?   30
Being "Salt Wise"   34

The Salt Kitchen
Salt Essentials   38
Layers of Flavour   50
Preserved   60
Most Appetising   72
From the Sea   80
The Main Course   92
Vegetables   104
Sauces   112
Sweet   122
From the Dairy   134

The Story of Salt
From the Source   148
The Means of Production   154
Raking in Profits   160
That Salty Taste   166
Saucy   172
Of Cabbages and Ham   178
Bread and Cheese   184
The Wisdom of Salt   190

Resources
Salts   198
Measurements and Conversions   202
Index of Recipes   203
Bibliography   206
Credits   206
Acknowledgements   206
My Tasting Notes   207

There is something magical about salt.

But it is a magic that is easy to overlook. Salt is so common, so familiar, that we barely notice the remarkable properties it possesses. The one thing we do notice, however, is its absence. As Thomas Keller, one of the world's great chefs, says, without salt the taste of food is flat…insipid. Salt makes flavours come alive, makes them "sparkle".

We don't even need our taste buds to confirm this: all we need to do is imagine. Imagine a dish of sirloin steak, French fries and fresh green beans. Then tell yourself that the steak is unseasoned, the fries unsalted and the beans cooked in plain water. For most of us, the very *idea* is unpalatable. Somehow it just isn't right—even in the imagination. That's the magic of salt.

There is more to it than simply making food taste better. The search for salt, its acquisition and trade, has been one of the driving forces of progress and civilisation. Indeed, without salt there is no life, because without salt our cells do not function. It is scarcely an exaggeration to say that without salt, we are nothing.

So it is little wonder that salt is everywhere. The art and the language of almost every culture is littered with references to salt. It is mentioned over 40 times in the King James Bible, and almost every religion uses, or has used, salt as part of its ritual. Salt cleanses, purifies, and wards off evil. Because it is immutable—its essence does not change—it has come to symbolise friendship, loyalty and fidelity. The covenant between God and the ancient Hebrews was seen to be eternal, and so it was symbolised by a substance that is eternal: salt.

Yet salt might seem to us anything but eternal. After all, if you drop it in water, does it not simply disappear?

Yes, it does. But if you wait long enough, the salt will always return.

Dissolve a teaspoonful of fine table salt in some warm water, then pour the liquid on to a plate or shallow bowl. Leave it in the sun. After a day, small crystals will start to form. In a few more days, all of the water will be gone; in its place will be a layer of pure, white salt.

What's more, it will seem to have multiplied—there will be at least 2 teaspoonsful of salt to return to the container.

Of course this is only an illusion, because although the salt has doubled in volume its weight is unchanged. The small, uniform crystals of refined table salt, formed on an industrial scale by huge vacuum evaporators, have been replaced by the large, irregular flakes that are the result of gradual solar evaporation.

The salt, however, remains the same.

The Mystery of Salt

Therein lies the paradox. If all salt is the same, how then can there be so many different varieties? If salt is truly essential to life, why are we being constantly advised to eat less of it? How much is too much?

For adults, the National Heart Foundation of Australia recommends a maximum intake of no more than 6 g (¼ oz)—approximately 1½ teaspoons of refined table salt—per day. At the same time it is acknowledged that around three quarters of the salt we consume comes from processed food. Salt that is virtually invisible.

As home cooks, we are confronted with a dizzying array of salts: Himalayan pink salt, Murray River salt, Indian black salt and *fleur de sel* are just a fraction of them. There are smoked salts, bamboo salts, flavoured salts, pickling salt and kosher salt. Each salt is subtly different, and each has its ideal application. To restrict ourselves to just one would be foolish. To deprive ourselves of the magic that salt brings to food would be something close to madness.

What we need is the right amount of the right salt for the right dish. By paying attention to the type of salt we use, and the way in which we use it, we can create food that simply tastes better. The fact that it will also be healthier is simply an added bonus.

Such is the way of salt. If its only important property was the enhancement of flavour, then we would need only a recipe book to tell its story. But a compound that has around 14,000 different uses requires something more. A compound that joins a reactive metal (which may spontaneously explode) with a greenish, poisonous gas to form a type of rock that human beings must consume to stay alive—this is a substance whose story needs telling in more detail.

Why do we habitually consume far more salt than our body requires? What makes some salt pink? Or grey? Why does salt make even sweet things taste better? And what, in fact, is salt?

Making Things Taste Better

In chemical terms, a *salt* is the product of a reaction between an acid and a base. Confusingly, what we call "salt" is not such a thing: it is a molecule made up of sodium (Na) and chloride (Cl) atoms. Its scientific name is sodium chloride (NaCl), but it has been known throughout the ages as common salt.

It is not the only salt we consume: there is calcium chloride and magnesium chloride in our diet, along with a host of other minerals. But only sodium chloride tastes salty.

And though it now seems hard to believe, our sense of taste is not there for our pleasure. Biologically, taste is a means for identifying potential toxins and essential nutrients in our food supply. The biological significance of sodium is reflected in the fact that one taste quality—*salty*—is solely dedicated to identifying foods that contain it. We need it, so we developed a taste for it.

Or rather, we didn't. We simply cannot eat salt by itself. Drinking salty water makes us vomit. Even those people suffering severe salt deficiency do not crave salt itself. Salt, or sodium, makes itself desirable by making other foods taste better.

As former *Vogue* food critic, Jeffrey Steingarten, writes in his book *The Man Who Ate Everything*, salt is essential to good food and good cooking. "It sharpens and defines the inherent flavours of foods and magnifies their natural aromas. Salt unites the diverse tastes in a dish, marries the sauce with the meat, and turns the pallid sweetness of vegetables into something complex and savory. Salt also deepens the color of most fruits and vegetables and keeps cauliflower white. Salt controls the ripening of cheese and improves its texture, strengthens the gluten in bread, and can preserve meat and fish, while transforming its texture. Cooked without salt, most dishes taste dull, lifeless, and lacking in complexity."

That is why we crave salt, and that is why this book exists: to help you use salt in the kitchen, and to help make your food taste better. To do that, you need to know the whole story.

The Rainbow-hued Rock

We find salt in all colours, shapes and sizes; as well as pure white, salt may be pink, grey, black or green. For salt truly is a rainbow-hued rock.

Every molecule of salt is in the form of a tiny, perfect cube, far too small to be seen by the naked eye. Yet every grain of salt is different. Its crystals may be tiny and uniform or irregular and large as pebbles. Industrial salt producers may supply up to 40 different grades or sizes of salt, while artisan saltmakers can provide flakes of salt seemingly light as snow.

So what makes one salt different from another?

The most obvious differences are the ones we can see: colour, texture and the size of the grains or flakes. We will also feel the difference—if we pinch it between our fingers it might be moist or dry, flaky or granular. And although sodium chloride has no odour, if the salt has been smoked, or flavoured with herbs or spices, we will perceive some fragrance.

Finally, most importantly, there will be differences in taste.

All salt will taste "salty", it is true, but each salt will be salty in a different way. It may be sharp or subtle. It may taste of minerals or of the sea. There may be a strong hint of sulphur or a subtle, smoky flavour.

Ultimately, so much about salt depends on where it comes from, how it is made and what has been done to it after the fact. In the section entitled "The Story of Salt" beginning on page 146, we will explore the forces that shape salt, accounting for its myriad forms, and discover how salt has shaped the world, physically, culturally, politically and economically.

To start you on your own journey into the world of salt, we would like to stress the importance of being "salt wise". It is hoped that the tools and information outlined in the "Salt Wise" section beginning on page 12 will enable all home cooks to salt wisely and well, without fear of oversalting.

Having familiarised yourself with the different types of salt, and perhaps having undertaken your own salt tasting, you will find a comprehensive set of recipes, techniques and tips in "The Salt Kitchen" beginning on page 36.

salt wise

opposite A selection of the salts featured in this book. For a key to the salts, see pages 198–201.

Know Your Salt

Salt comes in many forms, a fact that is profoundly important when it comes to cooking. Because a teaspoon of table salt will contain more salt by weight than a teaspoon of fleur de sel, it will therefore be saltier. This is why we need to know our salt.

To really get to *know* salt, you need to be familiar with it—how it tastes, how it feels —so that you are using the right amount for any given purpose. We recommend that you keep in your kitchen four basic salts, and that you get to know them thoroughly. That way you will always use them correctly.

You should have a good quality, natural sea salt for general purpose use. You should have some fine sea salt or iodised table salt for baking. You should have a soft mineral salt for your meat dishes and to enhance earthy umami flavours. You should have a fleur de sel, or some other fine-quality finishing salt, especially good for delicate fish dishes. And finally, a quantity of rock salt for baking meat or fish.

These are the essentials. They should be stored in covered containers, but kept close at hand: the general-purpose sea salt should be right next to your stove, so that it is *always* at hand. It is the salt you will be using most often, and the one of which you really need to get the *feel*. Frequently, you will be adding it by hand, a pinch at a time, so get to know what the pinch feels like between your fingers.

You should also know how much it weighs. As a general rule, a heaped teaspoon of flaky sea salt weighs around 4–5 g (¼ oz). A heaped tablespoon is around 12–14 g (½ oz). Weigh the salt you will be using most often, and see if these values are equivalent. You should also weigh out the same quantities of table salt; you will find that they are heavier.

Finally, you should taste the salt you will be using. There are details on how to conduct a salt tasting on page 22. Follow them, use your senses, explore the recipes in this book, and soon you will know your salt.

Once you are familiar with the basic salts, you may want to expand your range with one or two specialty salts, such as truffle-scented salt for your breakfast eggs or a hickory smoked salt for lamb dishes.

Fleur de Sel

Fleur de sel, the "flower of the salt", is the name used for salt that has been raked by hand from salt ponds surrounding certain villages in France, predominately those around Brittany, on the Atlantic coast, and in the Camargue on the Mediterranean. It is harvested from May to September, when artisan *paludiers* patiently wait as the shallow pools of water in the salt ponds evaporate, creating the prized salt crystals. It is a delicate art: excessive movement will cause the "flower" to sink to the bottom, so salt can only be collected when the weather is warm and winds are light. The ponds are the same ones where the coarser *sel gris* is harvested, but for every 40 kg (88 lb) of sel gris produced, only around 1.5 kg (3¼ lb) of fleur de sel is harvested. Each day a new layer of salt rises to the top of the pond, crystallising in delicate flakes that are scooped up by the *paludier* using a wide, flat board on the end of a long pole. Each day's harvest comprises one batch of fleur de sel. The salt itself is white, although it can acquire a pinkish hue, and has long been prized by chefs and gourmets for its high quality. Light, flaky and with a pure, slightly mineral taste, fleur de sel is perfect for finishing dishes, either in the kitchen or at the table.

Sea Salt

Sea salt is the generic term for unrefined or minimally refined salt, usually containing many of the trace minerals found in seawater as it has been naturally evaporated from a living ocean, sea or bay. Some of the more common sources for sea salt are the North Sea, the Mediterranean Sea and the Atlantic Ocean, particularly in France on the coast of Brittany, although sea salt can be made from the waters of any ocean, large or small.

Sea salt is typically unrefined, so the minerals it contains may include iron, calcium, magnesium, potassium, manganese, zinc and iodine. These contribute to its bright, pure, clean flavour, which many consider carries the tang of the ocean. Less delicate —and less expensive—than fleur de sel, sea salt is perhaps the ideal general-purpose salt, suitable for nearly all uses in the kitchen, particularly if you keep both a coarse and a fine-grained variety on hand.

Rock Salt

The term rock salt applies to any salt that has been mined from salt deposits on or under the ground. This definition may also apply to salt which has been extracted from underground deposits by dissolving it in water, pumping the brine to the surface and then precipitating the liquid back into salt. Rock salt comes in a variety of sizes and, because it is cheap, can be used for anything that requires salt in large quantities, such as baking anything in a bed of salt.

Table Salt

Table salt is is highly refined salt—usually between 95% and 99% pure sodium chloride—which has been created to a uniform size by mechanical evaporators. It is often iodised, and usually contains an anticaking agent to allow it to flow freely.

For much of the twentieth century, most homes had iodised table salt in their kitchen and nothing else. There remains a place for iodised table salt, mainly where it will not be used directly *on* food—the salting of cooking water, for example—or in baking, where its uniform size makes for accurate measuring (although a fine sea salt is preferable). The strong, sharp taste of table salt means that, given the wealth of alternatives, it should never be used at the table or as a finishing salt.

Grey Salt

Sel gris, grey salt, usually refers to the grey French sea salt that is hand harvested with wooden rakes in the traditional method. A moist, unrefined sea salt produced along most coastal areas of France, it is typified by a light grey, slightly purple tinge, which comes from the clay found in the salt flats.

Because it comes from France, sel gris is a little more expensive than local salt, but it is still an ideal all-purpose salt. It is unrefined, so it contains a range of minerals, and the evaporation process leaves it slightly moist, meaning it can be easily handled with your fingers. Learning to judge the amount of salt you are adding by how it feels is an essential skill in cooking, one that professional chefs learn early in their training.

A cheaper alternative to sel gris is Korean grey salt, which is available at many Asian supermarkets. It is similar in texture, colour and taste, though it will generally be drier than sel gris.

Pink Salt

Of all the colours that salt comes in, pink is definitely the most popular. Or at least the most common.

The colour comes either from the minerals that are bound in with the salt crystals, or from a salt-loving bacteria that produces a red carotenoid pigment, providing a valuable source of beta-carotene. Pink salts come most frequently from inland areas, where deposits have been left by the evaporation of prehistoric seas. Himalayan pink salt, Peruvian pink salt and Australia's Murry River pink salt are perhaps the three most popular varieties.

Both the Himalayan and the Peruvian salts are mined from pure salt deposits that lie high in the mountains, and they both possess the rich, mineral flavour that is common to pink salt. Because they are mined rather than evaporated, the crystals are substantial, and contribute a definite "crunch" to dishes on which they are used.

Murray River pink salt is sourced from an underground aquifer near Mildura, Victoria, which is pumped to the surface through the mineral-rich soil, absorbing nutrients as it goes. The brine is evaporated first by the sun, then mechanically, producing a uniform flake salt that is now used by chefs around the world.

Red, Black and Blue Salt

As we have seen, salt comes in most colours of the rainbow, and from all corners of the globe. Because pure salt is pure white or even translucent, the colours they gain are from natural elements incorporated into the salt crystals as they are produced.

Hawaiian 'Alaea salt is almost red; these salts take their name from the iron-oxide-rich red volcanic clay, called 'Alaea, that gives them colour. Harvested on the Hawaiian island of Kauai, which is their only source, these salts are claimed to have the highest concentration of trace minerals and elements of all salt. Authentic 'Alaea red clay will cause a fizzing reaction when added to a liquid, and imparts a subtle, mellow flavour to the salt. However, because clay and salt will separate in water, 'Alaea salt should be mainly used as a finishing salt.

Harvested from Iran, Persian Blue salt is a natural rock salt that is mineral rich with a hint of sweetness. It is dotted with blue crystals, which are in fact salt crystals that have been highly compressed, causing them to turn blue.

Also known as black salt or sanchal, *kala namak* is an unrefined volcanic table salt with a strong sulphuric flavour. Despite its name, kala namak, which is mined in Central India, is actually light pink in color. It is rich in minerals and most often used to flavour Indian dishes such as chaats and vegetable and fruit salads.

Smoked Salt

The effects of smoke on salt are quite remarkable: the smoke clings to the surface of the salt crystals, coating them with a rich, woody colour and imparting a strong, smoky flavour. And when the salt dissolves, that flavour goes straight into the food.

People have been smoking their salt since at least the time of the Vikings, who produced salt by evaporating seawater in a big vessel over an open, smoky fire containing juniper, cherry, elm, beech and oak woods.

In modern times, the salt is often produced first, then subsequently smoked. Both Maldon from England and Halen Môn in Wales produce a salt that has been smoked over oak wood, which goes especially well with roasted meat. The type of wood used has a distinct effect on the flavour: salt smoked over chardonnay oak wine barrels, for example, will achieve a gentle smoke flavour with a savory hint of wine.

Similar in concept to smoked salt is *jook yeom*, a Korean salt made by roasting sea salt in bamboo cylinders plugged with yellow mud. The salt absorbs minerals from the bamboo and mud, which in turn leach the salt of impurities. Many Koreans use bamboo salt for its nutritional value and as an aid for indigestion.

Flavoured Salt

There are many flavoured salts on the market now, but the best ones to buy are those that you would be unable to make yourself.

Perhaps the best of these is truffle salt, a touch of which will turn even the most ordinary dish into something special—try it on creamy scrambled eggs and you'll find that breakfast has transformed into an indulgent treat.

Vanilla salt is also very useful to have in the cupboard: you will be surprised how many things it will enliven, from fruit to seafood. And many salt companies sell prepared combinations of salt, herbs and spices to use as the basis of rubs and marinades. Just be aware that, unlike ordinary salt, these flavoured salts will not last forever, so buy them in quantities you know that you will use.

And of course, there is always chicken salt. There are few Australians who don't occasionally (or indeed frequently) find themselves craving chips with chicken salt, so it can't hurt to keep a container handy!

The Himalayan Salt Block

Cut from slabs of solid crystal salt, the Himalayan salt block is an innovative way to add salt to the cooking (or curing) process. The block may be chilled to freezing point or heated to 230°C (445°F), making it ideal for serving hot or cold foods.

The blocks are carved from slabs of pure salt that is estimated to be up to 250 million years old. They look a little like pink marble, but one touch with the tongue confirms that they are indeed made of salt. They can be used as serving platters, to cure food and to cook it. And, not just savoury dishes: a chilled block can be used for tempering chocolate, setting caramel or even for creating a dramatic fruit *flambé* to present at the table.

Although salt blocks will sustain temperatures from -18°C (-0.4°F) to over 450°C (840°F), it is best to reserve one block for each purpose. Those that have been subject to heat will change their appearance as a result, becoming more tempered and less suitable for presentation. The salt block must also be heated SLOWLY. This can be done in the oven or on the stove top, but care should be taken to avoid it touching electric elements. The salt block should also be carried very carefully when hot, particularly if it has developed any cracks.

Innovations

The salt block is but one innovation in salting. The way we apply salt to food is open to our imaginations.

We know that, where possible, we should be sparing with our salt use. It has been suggested that our palates become inured to over-seasoned food, and that we can train our tastes back in the opposite direction. One solution is that in the kitchen we salt lightly—just enough to bring out the flavours—and provide diners with the opportunity to add just a little more, but not too much, at the table.

An ideal way to salt lightly is the Sea Breeze. Simply take a small atomiser bottle, add a little salt and then fill with warm water. Shake to dissolve the salt, and let the water cool. This salted water is a great way to season certain foods, particularly vegetables, with a light, even touch of salt that will not overwhelm them.

In reducing salt consumption, dieticians also recommend tempering salt with a little citric acid. An interesting way of doing this is to combine salt and lemon juice in one parcel. Simply cut a lemon in half, then sprinkle the cut surface with some coarse sea salt. Take a small square of muslin and wrap that around the lemon, twist the ends and tie with string. This becomes the perfect vehicle for salting not just seafood but many other dishes. The lemon juice will dissolve the salt, and your food will recieve a salty, citrus tang that can be used sparingly, but still to great effect.

Jan Gundlach, Director of Flavours at the Culinary Centre in Canberra, Australia, says, "The wise application of salt and spices has unrealised culinary potential, and only by consciously tasting different salts and by seasoning with precision can we elevate food to unknown flavour dimensions and still control our daily intake of sodium chloride."

opposite Gravlax salmon (recipe page 66) served on a Himalayan pink salt slab, with Cyprus black salt and a salted lemon wrapped in muslin.

Tasting Salt

Why do we need to taste salt? Surely all salt tastes the same? That is, salty.

In fact, different types of salt have subtly different flavours. This is a result of a number of factors: the mineral content of the salt, its method of production, the size and shape of the crystals, and whether it has had any flavourings added to it.

The only way to truly gauge the unique flavours of different salts is to taste each of them individually, to taste them in comparison with other salts, and to taste different salts in combination with a range of foods, to see which salt goes best with what.

The first thing to do is to acquire some salt. These should be the salts that will be in your kitchen on a permanent basis, along with a few specialty salts. Remember, for one of life's essentials, salt is still cheap, so you can afford to experiment with some of the more exotic salts as well as the basics. Before you begin tasting, make sure you have some unsalted crackers and some water with a little lemon squeezed in it to "cleanse" your palate between tastes.

The easiest method of tasting is to put some salt in the middle of your palm, pinch a little between your fingers and then taste it with the tip of your tongue. This will give you an idea of both the flavour and the texture. Cleanse your palate, then move on. Each salt will have a different effect, and it may help to keep notes as you go, so you remember what you tasted.

The next method is tasting in solution. By weight, measure out equivalent amounts of each salt. Measure by weight and not by volume, because the different grain size and shape in the various salts result in different amounts of salt per unit of volume.

You won't need much, so use the smallest measurement you can. Mix each kind of salt with enough hot water to make a 2–3% solution. Let the solutions cool and taste them. This will give an idea of the "pure" salt taste, unaffected by the crystal size, which governs the way the salt dissolves on the tongue.

The final method, and no doubt the most enjoyable, is to prepare a range of different foods, divided into small portions, with which to compare and contrast the different salts as they affect flavour. A good selection would be:

Tomato
Hard-boiled egg
Melon
Cucumber
Grapefruit
Rare beef
Chocolate

Cut each of the foods into small pieces and lay them out on plates. Put all of the salts you have into small dishes—make sure you know which one is which—and then start. Put a little of two different types of salt on the same type of food. Compare the difference; you will be surprised at how much difference there is. Cleanse your palate with a piece of cracker and some water, then try two further salts on the same type of food. Remember to write down your thoughts. Then try the same type of salt on two different types of food. As you go along you will come to see—or rather, taste—that salts are different, and that some salts taste better on certain foods than others.

At the Table

Finding new ways to present salt at the table helps to make diners salt conscious, and it is a great way to add a talking point to your meals. The combination of colours, textures and flavours that salt can provide makes for endless possibilities. But first, you need to throw out your salt shaker.

opposite Fruit paired with salt for a salt tasting. Salts (from the top): truffle salt, macrobiotic sea salt, Netherlands smoked salt, Hawaiian 'Alaea salt and Murray River pink salt.

above Ideas for presenting salt include the "sea breeze" (left) and a piece of Himalayan pink salt paired with a small grater.

opposite As you add salts to your repertoire, you will find new ways to present them at the table.

opposite A presentation of Japanese salts: bonito salt (top left), hibiscus salt (top right) and squid ink salt (bottom).

above Salt presented on decorative spoons: Netherland smoked salt (top left), Hawaiian 'Alaea salt (top right), Himalayan pink salt (centre) and Maldon sea salt (bottom left).

Too Much?

One level teaspoon of refined table salt weighs approximately 4 g (⅛ oz). By this measure, the average European in the eighteenth century was consuming *18* teaspoons of salt every day.

It's an astounding number, not of itself, but in comparison to the *1* teaspoon of salt that the National Heart Foundation of Australia recommends as an upper limit for individuals with high blood pressure, or the upper limit of 1½ teaspoons recommended for all Australians.

The Foundation also recommends that governments set a target for reducing the average salt consumption of adults to less than 6 g (¼ oz) a day in 2010, and develop a social marketing campaign to increase Australians' awareness of the importance of reducing salt consumption.

The reason, as the Foundation's position statement on electrolytes states, is that: "There is moderate evidence in the scientific literature to indicate that high dietary sodium intake is associated with increased stroke incidence, and mortality from coronary heart disease and CVD [cardiovascular disease]." The statement also gives acknowledgment that: "Further studies are needed to clarify the evidence that reducing dietary sodium is associated with a reduced risk of CVD."

Australian adults currently eat about 9 g (⅜ oz)—2¼ teaspoons—of salt per day.

This is eight times less than the amount of salt consumed by eighteenth-century Europeans. Yet there is little evidence to suggest that in the eighteenth century rates of cardiovascular disease were eight times higher.

How Much is Too Much?

We do have evidence that there is a link between sodium and blood pressure. It was first noticed in 1904 by two French doctors, who had six hospital patients with high blood pressure. The doctors, Ambard and Beaujard, observed that their patient's blood pressure improved when salt was removed from their diet, then rose again when they were served a salty soup.

Multiple studies since then have indicated the same thing, and those quoted by the National Heart Foundation of Australia show definable reductions in blood pressure when dietary sodium intake is reduced.

Obesity and alcohol consumption are also associated with high blood pressure, as is diabetes. Age, too, is a factor.

And while there are no absolute clinical rules about what is defined as high blood pressure, commonly accepted guidelines define hypertension as blood pressure that is equal to or more than a systolic pressure of 140 mm Hg and a diastolic pressure of 90 mm Hg. Equal to, or more than, 180/110 and you have very high blood pressure. People with high blood pressure are more likely to develop heart disease and stroke.

The Homeostatic Organism

A book published in 2004 by Dr Trevor C Beard called *Salt Matters: A Consumer Guide* was reprinted in 2007. Only the title had changed, and the book is now called *Salt Matters: The Killer Condiment*.

In it, Dr Beard says: "Salt matters because a massive international consensus blames it [salt] for many serious health problems. High blood pressure is by far the most important of these—it has become the greatest epidemic of non-infectious disease ever to affect the human race—and the other problems are by no means negligible."

Dr Beard strongly advocates a low-salt diet. He also states that many people with a raised blood pressure "find they can control their blood pressure without drugs— sometimes indefinitely—by adopting a healthier diet and lifestyle. They...can increase the benefits of this action by controlling their weight, taking regular exercise, eating more fruit and vegetables than is usual in industrialised societies, limiting alcohol and managing stress."

The human body is a homeostatic system, which means that each part both affects, and is regulated by, every other part. It is a system that has evolved over two million years to consume a diet that bears little relation to the way we eat now: the introduction of diets high in sugar and refined carbohydrates has had a profound effect on the health of industrialised societies. American science writer Gary Taubes, in his book *Good Calories, Bad Calories*, calls hypertension "a disease of civilisation", and quotes geneticist James Neel (speaking particularly of adult-onset diabetes) that: "The changing dietary patterns of Western civilisation had compromised a complex homeostatic mechanism."

Taubes' argument, echoed by many, is that there are various nutritional explanations for the rise in blood pressure that accompanies Western diets and lifestyles, and that any insistence that salt is the cause of hypertension and the increase in blood pressure which accompanies ageing yet which fails to look at associated dietary factors is perhaps too limited.

What's more, Taubes says: "Systematic reviews of the evidence, whether published by those who believe salt is responsible for hypertension or by those who don't, have inevitably concluded that significant reductions in salt consumption—cutting our average salt intake in half, for instance, which is difficult to accomplish in the real world—will drop blood pressure by perhaps 4–5 mm Hg in hypertensives and 2 mm Hg in the rest of us."

But even though the values appear small, argues Dr Keast, such reductions in blood pressure are calculated to have significant population effects on the incidence of stroke and ischemic heart disease.

The Invisible Salt

The standard study of where our dietary salt actually comes from was performed in Scotland and published in 1987. It states that 75% of the salt in the diet of industrialised societies comes from processed food, 10% is the salt which naturally occurs in food, and the remaining 15% is added during cooking or at the table.

So it is easy to see how anybody wishing to reduce their sodium intake could achieve this, simply by avoiding all processed food. In the words of Dr. Trevor Beard, "the robust health and vigour of the world's salt-free societies provides abundant evidence that fresh foods provide all the salt we need for perfect health."

But we must acknowledge that actually doing it is probably not so simple. Processed food is ubiquitous, and its pleasures can be very hard to resist. The problem is that, as Dr. Keast says, the salt within processed food is "invisible" to the tongue and the eye. For example, a report published in 2009 found that more than two-thirds of pizzas sold by takeaway chains and supermarkets in Australia contained twice the daily recommended amount of salt for adults. One pizza contained 13 g (½ oz) of salt.

Fortunately, food labelling standards require that almost all processed food has its sodium content listed. To work out how much salt is in any given food requires only a simple calculation. Because the figure for sodium is given in milligrams (mg) per serve, one simply multiplies the quantity per serving by 0.0025 to arrive at the amount of salt.

If there is 870 mg of sodium in each serving, then the sum is 870 x 0.0025, which equals 2.175 g of salt.

If one already has the specific health problems associated with high blood pressure, diabetes, obesity or cardiovascular disease, comprehensive salt-watching is recommended. And it must be remembered that the effect of dietary salt is chronic, not acute; as we live longer, those chronic effects build up, and so become a major cause of diet-related disease for people between ages of 60 and 80 years. Salt may be an essential nutrient, but it will also kill prematurely if consumed to excess.

Being "Salt Wise"

It is generally agreed that too much salt is bad for us. Yet salt is essential for life. Furthermore, salt improves the taste of virtually every food we eat, so long as it is applied in the right amount. The difference between too much and too little, both in terms of what's good for our bodies and what's good for our food, is a very fine line. We may cross it without even knowing.

But there is a way in which we can do what's best for our food and our health, both at the same time. To do that, we need to be "salt wise".

Know Your Salt

We need to be aware of the salt that we eat. We need to know how salt tastes, and if we have used too much or too little. We need to use the right salt, in the right amount, for the right dish. That is being "salt wise".

Abandon the Shaker

We need to know how salt feels. When cooking with salt we need to use our fingers and hands to add salt in small increments, tasting as we go, to ensure that we neither oversalt nor undersalt.

We need to throw out the salt shaker: when salting food at the table, we need to use better salt more sparingly, rather than shaking table salt with abandon. That is being "salt wise".

Be Aware of "Hidden" Salt

We need to know that over three-quarters of the salt in our diet comes from processed food rather than food we cook at home. We need to read food labels, and make a conscious decision to choose foods that are lower in sodium.

We need to acknowledge the Heart Foundation of Australia's recommendations of a maximum of 6 g (¼ oz) of salt per day for adults—roughly 1 heaped teaspoon—and strive to keep within those guidelines. That is being "salt wise".

Take Some Iodine

We need to consume some iodine. Iodine is essential for the healthy function of the thyroid gland, which produces hormones that regulate metabolism, including the regulation of body temperature. The daily iodine requirement for most adults is 150 micrograms.

In Australia and New Zealand, the governments have mandated that iodised salt will be used in the production of bread at an average level of 4.5 mg of iodine per 100 g (3½ oz) of salt. We need to consume products that have been made with iodised salt, or add a small amount of iodised salt to our own cooking. That is being "salt wise".

Read the Label

We need to know how to read a label.

We need to know that on nutrition labels salt is expressed as sodium. We need to know that sodium is Na and salt is NaCl.

To calculate the amount of salt, we need to multiply the amount of sodium by 2.5.

Therefore:

milligrams of sodium (Na) × 2.5
= milligrams of salt (NaCl)

For example, 200 mg of sodium equates to 500 mg or 0.5 g of salt (200 mg × 2.5 = 500 mg salt or 0.5 g).

To convert milligrams of salt to milligrams of sodium we need to divide the salt content by 2.5.

Nutrition information panels will show "per serve" and "per 100 g (3½ oz)" columns. We should always make our calculations based on sodium per 100 g (3½ oz).

The Heart Foundation recommends products that have a sodium below 120 mg/100 g (3½ oz). We should use this as a guide.

We need to know that some products we would think have little added salt—because they are not salty—actually contain very high levels of salt. The value of sodium in bread (1200 mg/100g [3½ oz]) and breakfast cereals is an example.

We should know the amount of sodium contained in the processed foods we eat. That is being "salt wise".

Eat Well

Most importantly, we need to eat well. We need to take the time to prepare food for ourselves which is healthy, tasty and ecologically viable. We need to season that food sparingly, with quality salt that is made using natural processes. We need to use the right salt, in the right amount, for the right dish. That is being "salt wise". And only if you are "salt wise" can you eat well.

NUTRITION INFORMATION			
Servings per package: 8 Serving size: Approx. 56 g			
	Average Quantity per serving	% Daily Intake* (per serving)	Average Quantity per 100 g (3½ oz)
Energy	611 kJ (131 Cal)	7.0%	1090 kJ (261 Cal)
Protein	5.6 g	11.2%	10.0 g
Fat, total – saturated	6.4 g 2.6 g	9.1% 10.8%	11.5 g 4.6 g
Carbohydrate	15.5 g	5.0%	27.7 g
– sugars	3.1 g	3.4%	5.6 g
Sodium	274 mg	11.9%	490 mg

*Percentage Daily Intakes are based on an average adult diet of 8700 kJ. Your daily intake may be higher or lower depending on your energy needs.

above A typical frozen pizza label, chosen at random. This pizza contains 490 mg of sodium per 100 g (3½ oz), which equals 1.225 g of salt.

the salt kitchen

opposite The perfect steak (see recipe on page 94) begins with a layer of coarse sea salt, which is brushed off before the steak is cooked.

Salt Essentials

A pot, a flame, a knife and some salt. These are the essentials; anything else is a bonus. Conversely, if we remove any of these four elements then cooking—preparing food that tastes good—becomes almost impossible.

Preparing food that tastes good. Preparing food that *is* good. This is of such singular importance that we should not even have to think about it. It should just *be*.

Unfortunately, we live in a world where the food we eat is frequently precooked, prepackaged and, for us, often preparation-free. Food is produced on an industrial scale, and those processes which people have used every day over many centuries for preparing and preserving food have become obscure, mysterious even, to the average person. The simple act of making salt—a process that for millennia has been essential for continued human existence—is something that very few of us have done for ourselves.

But why make salt? Why cure our own ham, make our own butter or cheese or ice cream, when all we need to do is go to the supermarket and pick them off the shelves?

Perhaps, just because we can. Because there is so much satisfaction—and so many savings and benefits—to be gained from doing it ourselves. Because many of the health issues faced by the Western world are attributable to the things we eat, and if we make our own food, we can more easily control what goes into our bodies.

Or perhaps simply because cooking is enjoyable. Fun. Exciting, even. And because most of us only cook the food we like to eat, we are sure to savour the results.

In the following pages there is much to savour: from sweet cured ham to salted caramel macarons, Thai dipping sauce to *dulce de leche*. Some of the recipes, like those for bread and baking, should be followed precisely. Others are little more than suggestions as to how something might be best prepared. But all of them, really, should be considered mostly as a leaping-off point from which to explore a range of different foods and techniques.

Keeping it Clean

A number of these techniques are to do with preserving. The point of preserving food is to keep naturally occurring bad bacteria from running wild and spoiling the food. It stands to reason, then, that we should seek to exclude as much of these bacteria from the process as possible.

At the same time, there may be naturally occurring good bacteria that we seek to encourage, and we need to make room for them to thrive.

Salt is naturally an antibacterial agent; that is why it works to preserve food. Yet sometimes salt, in quantities that are palatable, may not be enough. Hygiene is essential. Containers and utensils must be scrupulously clean. Jars need to be sterilised, and if they are to be sealed the seal must be uncompromised.

Mostly, though, it is a matter of common sense. If everything is kept clean and temperatures are appropriate, things will generally be fine. If your food is contaminated it will usually be obvious—trust your eyes, and your nose. And if there's any doubt, as they say, throw it out.

Just the Beginning

Salt's preservative powers make it invaluable. The fact that it is both essential to life *and* nature's supreme flavour enhancer makes it indispensable. And while a kitchen without salt is not really a kitchen, a kitchen with salt is an entire world. Its possibilities are endless—these recipes are just the beginning. Take them as your inspiration, and those possibilities will be revealed.

opposite Cyprus black salt adds unexpected drama to bread and unsalted butter.

Sea Salt

Although the variety of salt available to us seems virtually limitless, we do not *have* to buy our salt. Anyone with access to the ocean can make their own salt: the process is simple, yet somehow very satisfying.

Strain the seawater through a sieve lined with muslin to remove any impurities. Put the seawater into a large pot and boil until it is reduced by three-quarters. Leave to cool.

Transfer the brine to one or more wide shallow dishes—greater surface area will result in quicker evaporation—and leave in a warm place, preferably in direct sunlight, until most of the brine has evaporated. Scrape the sides and the bottom of the container, bringing the salt crystals into what remains of the brine. Leave in direct sunlight, stirring occasionally, until the crystals are completely dry.

For every 4 l (8½ pints) of seawater you will get approximately 150 g (5¼ oz) of salt. The salt may taste slightly tangy and even vaguely sweet, which is due to the minerals that are trapped, along with some seawater, inside the crystals.

Common sense tells us that seawater from inner-city beaches or anywhere close to potential contamination is to be avoided. Conversely, water from any ocean source that has regular tidal flow and is away from any obvious source of contaminants should be perfectly safe.

Homemade Salt

Even if you do not have access to the sea, you can still make your own salt. The different flavours of salt are a product not only of the minerals (or lack thereof) they contain, but also the shape of the crystals themselves. Ordinary table salt's sharp taste is as much to do with its size and shape—being produced by rapid evaporation under high pressure—as its purity.

Dissolve the salt in the water. Pour the brine onto a plate and set it in the sun. Occasionally scrape the small crystals that form at the edges of the plate back into the brine. Within three or four days all of the liquid will have evaporated and the salt will be ready to use.

If you are unsure whether your table salt is iodised, don't worry, it will be easy to tell; the iodine will begin to precipitate first, leaving a yellow crust around the edges of the brine. Obviously this is not only harmless but beneficial —simply scrape the iodine crystals back into the salt and they will all but disappear.

2 large red chillies	
100 g (3½ oz) sea salt	

Smoked Chilli Salt

Smoked salt is an incredible condiment, and it is surprisingly simple to create. If you do not have a smoker, one can easily be improvised: all you need is a wok and a wire rack that will fit inside it.

First, line the wok with aluminium foil, then put a layer of smoking wood chips in the bottom—any hard wood will do, particularly fruit woods such as apple or cherry, or you can make your own by sawing up any small piece of oak or hickory and collecting the sawdust. Sit the wire rack in the wok, put a quantity of good quality sea salt in a heatproof container and then cover the wok with foil and then a tight-fitting lid. Put the wok over the heat, making sure that the wood chips only smoke and do not catch fire.

You can smoke salt by itself, of course, but it is even better when spiced with a little chilli.

Slice the chillies, then place in a mortar with the salt. Grind the two together roughly, then place in a heatproof container. Put the mixture in the smoker and smoke for 30 minutes. Allow to cool, then rub together with your hands to blend the flavours. Transfer to covered container and store in the refrigerator.

To make different varieties of smoked salt, it is best to mix the flavourings through the salt before you smoke it. Not all flavoured salts will work in combination with the smoke—celeriac is definitely one that does, as are porcini mushrooms and Sichuan peppercorns. Experiment to see what succeeds.

Cayenne Salt

Cayenne Salt
50 g (1¾ oz) dried birds-eye chillies
2 tablespoons sea salt
1 glass of white wine
2 glasses of water

Cayenne Salt

Once you realise that salt will always recrystallise, you can begin to add other flavourings to brine to produce useful and interesting variations. The following is a recipe from the *Indian Domestic Economy and Receipt Book*, Madras 1850, reprinted in Elizabeth David's *Spices, Salt and Aromatics in the English Kitchen*.

"Take two ounces of finely powdered dried birds-eye chillies or capsicums, and mix them well in a mortar with two table-spoonfuls of clean salt; add a glass of white wine and two of water; put it into a corked bottle, and place in the sun for a week or more daily; then strain the whole through a fine piece of muslin; pour the liquor in a plate, and then evaporate it either by a stove or in the sun; you will then have crystals of cayenne and salt; a much finer article than the cayenne powder."

Almost anything that is liquid or can be dissolved may be used to flavour salt: as in the previous recipe, you should aim for around equal parts of salt and the flavouring ingredient. Things you might like to try could include red wine, lime juice, balsamic vinegar, tabasco or even coffee. Dilute them with enough warm water to dissolve the salt, then follow the above procedure, or simply strain directly into a shallow dish and place in the sun.

Spice Salts

Spices are the ideal thing for enlivening salt, and almost any combination of spices can be added to salt, either simply by shaking the two together, or grinding them in a mortar or spice grinder. Remember, if you are using seeds, it is best to lightly toast them before grinding to bring out the flavour.

When making flavoured salt, it is better to make quantities that can be used within two weeks; any longer and they will begin to lose their flavour. Base your quantities around 50 g (1¾ oz)—about 4 heaped tablespoons—of good quality sea salt, and keep them in a covered container in the refrigerator for maximum freshness.

Salt and pepper: it is virtually one word. Here is a simple way to keep them both together in the one place, giving you a spicy, aromatic salt that will enhance everything it touches.

Sichuan Salt

50 g (1¾ oz) sea salt

1½ teaspoons Sichuan peppercorns

Crush the peppercorns roughly in a mortar. Remove any husks, then toast lightly in a heavy saucepan over a medium heat. Lower the heat and add the salt, shaking the pan regularly. The salt will begin to colour slightly. Remove from the heat, cool, then grind briefly in the mortar to incorporate.

—

This classic Japanese seasoning has an enlivening effect on rice dishes, over eggs and in miso soup, among other things.

Gomashio

7 tablespoons white sesame seeds

1 tablespoon sea salt

Use the same procedure as for Sichuan salt. An interesting addition to this salt is seaweed; toast a couple of sheets of nori over an open flame and grind it in with the sesame seeds. You could also add a pinch of dried chilli flakes.

—

The unique, aniseed aroma of star anise is not for everybody, but there are certain foods for which it is the perfect spice note. Adding it in the form of salt will mean that the flavour is never overpowering.

Aniseed Salt

50 g (1¾ oz) sea salt

5 star anise

Lightly toast the star anise, then grind it in a mortar or a spice grinder. Add the sea salt and mix to incorporate.

—

Of course you can make the above salts in quantities smaller than the recipes above, if you want a special salt just for one particular dish. You can also use powdered spices, if you desire, and simply stir a pinch through a teaspoonful of sea salt. And it hardly needs to be said that there is no limit to the variety of spiced salts you can create.

Herb Salts

As with spices, almost any type of herb may be used to flavour salt. Again, make small quantities so as to retain the maximum flavour, and store covered in the refrigerator.

This is possibly the perfect seasoning for steak. In fact, it is possibly the perfect seasoning for *anything*.

Tarragon Salt

50 g (1¾ oz) sea salt	
Small bunch of tarragon	

Chop the tarragon finely and mix with the salt. Keep in a covered container in the refrigerator.

Potatoes are just the beginning for this salt, although there are few foods whose taste it will not improve.

Rosemary Salt

50 g (1¾ oz) sea salt	
1 small handful of rosemary	

Roughly chop the rosemary and then grind it in a mortar with the salt to release its oils.

Salt will absorb flavours through contact, so you can mix it with things that you would not normally eat.

Lavender Salt

50 g (1¾ oz) sea salt	
2–3 stems of lavender	

Put the salt with the lavender in a plastic bag, and leave for a few days; it will gradually absorb the aroma of the lavender. Leave them together in the bag, using the salt as required.

Salts made with herbs will often be a little damp, due to the essential oils that herbs release as they are crushed. If the salt is going to be used for sprinkling, it can be dried by leaving it in the sun, or in a warm oven, stirring occasionally with your fingers. And, as with all the previous salts, virtually any type of herb can be used, from curry leaf to chervil, fennel or horseradish, caraway or lemon verbena.

Combination Salts

You can use salt as the base for accumulating multiple flavours. Simply choose a particular theme—Indian, say, or Mediterranean, or citrus—and add a range of complementary herbs, spices and aromatics.

This recipe shows exactly how the right herbs, spices and salt can come together to form an harmonious whole. It is taken from Justin North's excellent book, *Becasse*.

Aromatic Salt

100 g (3½ oz) sea salt
½ cinnamon stick
2 garlic cloves
4 sprigs thyme
1 sprig rosemary
1 small bay leaf
1 star anise
2 white peppercorns
4 coriander (cilantro) seeds

Put all of the ingredients in a large mortar and pound until they form a coarse paste. Transfer to an airtight container and keep in the refrigerator. It will be good for about two weeks.

This combination of salt, citrus and sugar is perfect on any type of fish or seafood. It is based on a recipe from *Salt and Pepper* by Jody Vassallo.

Spicy Citrus Salt

75 g (2½ oz) sea salt
6 kaffir lime leaves
1 teaspoon chilli flakes
1 tablespoon dried lemon grass
1 teaspoon grated palm sugar

With a knife, shred the kaffir lime leaves. Process them in a spice grinder with the chilli and the lemon grass until finely chopped. Add this to the salt, along with the palm sugar, and mix well.

The above salts will be a little damp, like moist sand, and are ideal as a rub for meat or fish—simply add a little olive oil and a splash of red wine vinegar until they reach the required consistency. But if you would prefer them dry for sprinkling, just spread the salt in a baking tray and leave in a warm oven for 15 minutes to dry out, stirring occasionally.

Different combinations of flavours will evoke the cuisines of other countries. This spicy Indian-style salt is strong, so use it sparingly.

Spicy Indian Marinade

1 tablespoon sea salt
1 teaspoon ground turmeric
1 teaspoon ground coriander (cilantro)
1 teaspoon cumin seeds
1 teaspoon black mustard seeds
1 teaspoon garam masala
½ teaspoon cayenne pepper

Combine all the ingredients in a bowl and stir to mix thoroughly. Store in a covered container in the refrigerator. You can also stir through 4–5 tablespoons of yoghurt, and use this mixture as a marinade.

Exotic Salts

Exotic salts are those that you would not expect to use every week, or that might be required for a specific dish. That said, once you have made vanilla salt and tasted it on fruit or seafood, you are unlikely to want to be without it.

Because of its usefulness, vanilla salt can be made in greater quantity than other salts.

Vanilla Salt

100 g (3½ oz) sea salt
1 vanilla pod

Split the vanilla pod and scrape out the seeds. Mix them with the salt, then put the salt and the vanilla pod into a sealed container and leave in the refrigerator.

Whenever you buy a piece of fruit from a roadside stall in Thailand it will be accompanied by a small paper sachets of this salt mixture. One taste of it, sprinkled over mango, pineapple, pear or indeed any fruit at all, will show you why.

Prik-kab-klua

2 tablespoons sugar
1 tablespoon salt
2 fresh red chillies, sliced

Grind the ingredients in a small mortar; the chillies will tint the mixture a light pink, and their oil will give it the texture of wet sand. Serve with fresh fruit.

Like vanilla salt, this coconut salt will surprise you with how versatile it is.

Coconut Salt

2 tablespoons shredded coconut
100 g (3½ oz) sea salt

In a mortar, roughly grind the coconut before adding the salt. Mix thoroughly, then store in a covered container in the refrigerator.

The earthy taste of porcini combines with salt to provide a fantastic seasoning for all kinds of meat and game. This, too, comes from Justin North's *Becasse* cookbook.

Porcini Salt

100 g (3½ oz) sea salt
20 g (¾ oz) dried porcini mushrooms

Mix the salt and the porcini mushrooms together. Spread them in an even layer over a baking tray. Set the oven to its lowest temperature and dry the salt for 1–2 hours, then tip it into a bowl and rub together with your fingers to blend the flavours. Store in a covered container in the refrigerator.

As with all of the preceding salts, the only limit is your willingness to experiment. Try green apple salt, or pineapple salt, or lemon grass salt. And remember, pretty much anything goes!

Layers of Flavour

The most important thing to remember is that salt *changes* flavour, sometimes subtly, sometimes profoundly. Every time you add salt to food you should be conscious of this fact. Salt should be added regularly, in small amounts, at different stages of the cooking process, rather than all at once at the end.

This approach is in line with what is perhaps the most fundamental rule of cooking: *taste as you go*. One of a chef's most important tools is the spoon they carry with them at all times to dip into sauces, creams, stocks and soups, tasting everything at every stage to ensure that it is just right.

By layering salt and the addition of salty ingredients—stocks, salted oil, bacon, soy sauce, anchovies—you can ensure that your food is never *salty*, but always perfectly *salted*. And that is the foundation of good cooking.

Basic Soffrito

onions	
garlic	
salt	
oil	

Basic Soffrito

When at the stove, chefs rarely measure salt with anything other than their fingers. They know their salt by the way it *feels*. They know, too, that good cooking is a matter of layering flavours, and that each layer of flavour should be salted.

The first layer for many dishes is the *soffrito*, the basic components of which are onions and garlic. To these may be added diced celery and/or carrot. When you combine carrots, onions, celery and raw ham or bacon you have a *mirepoix*.

Use a large, sharp chef's knife. Slice the onion in half and remove the skin, place the cut side down, then cut vertical slices 3–4 mm (⅛ in) apart almost to the root, but not cutting all the way through. Hold on to the root end, turn the onion 90 degrees and slice thinly to make dice.

Peel the garlic, then slice finely. Using a rocking motion, roughly chop the garlic. Sprinkle with salt, then use the flat of the knife to crush the garlic against the chopping board; the salt will act as an abrasive, releasing the garlic juice and making it easier to crush.

Heat some oil in a frying pan over a low heat and add the onions and the garlic, stirring regularly. Do not allow to colour. Use as a base for soups, casseroles, sauces etc.

Both the soffrito and the mirepoix illustrate an essential fact of cooking; that salt will make its way into a dish through many channels. Whether it has been used to crush the garlic or comes with the addition of a salty ingredient such as ham, salt will generally accumulate in a dish as it is being cooked. Therefore, it is vital that you taste as you go.

Salted Water

Ideally, water for cooking pasta and vegetables should be as salty as seawater, around 3% solution. Dried pasta has a relatively long cooking time, and so loses a lot of flavour, which is why it needs a lot of salt. Eggs, too, should be cooked in salted water; not because it prevents the shells from cracking, but because the salt permeates the shell and imparts flavour to what would otherwise be a tasteless material.

Of course the most common use for salted water is for boiling vegetables. Here, the salt speeds the softening process, weakening the cell walls and releasing water pressure inside the cells, allowing the vegetables to become tender. Unsalted cooking water will draw out the natural salts and sugars from the vegetables' cells, diminishing the flavour of the vegetables.

Dissolve the salt in the water. This will give you cooking water that is appropriate for boiling pasta, vegetables, eggs, etc.

There has long been debate about when to add salt to the water: before or after it has begun to boil. In truth, it doesn't matter—if you add salt to water that is already boiling it will cool down, because the water loses energy in dissolving the salt, as well as increasing the mass of fluid to be heated. Still, the amount of time and energy required to boil salted water remains almost exactly the same as boiling unsalted water and then adding salt.

Stock

We are accustomed to pouring our cooking water down the sink, thinking that its job is done. But in doing so we are wasting both flavour and nutrients. As the cooking process breaks down the cellular structure of both meat and vegetables, a portion of their goodness is released into the water. If that water has been salted it will have a distinct flavour once the vegetables have been cooked. And if it is plain water in which something salty has been boiled—a ham, for example—it is has become, almost by accident, a lightly flavoured meat stock.

Depending on what has been cooked in the water, it will carry various flavours. To intensify these flavours, evaporate the water by boiling until it has been reduced by three-quarters. Let it cool and then freeze it in ice trays. Thaw these any time you are making a stock and add them to the process.

Most classic stocks are made without the addition of salt; they are often used in reduced form as a base for sauces, and it becomes difficult to gauge the level of saltiness the finished sauce will have. If your stocks are going to be used as the basis for casseroles, braises and sauces that are not highly reduced, it is not a problem.

Dashi
15 cm (6 in) piece of konbu
25 g (⅞ oz) bonito flakes
1.5 l (3¼ pint) water

Dashi

The Japanese stock, or *dashi*, is little more than salted water, getting its flavour from the sea itself in the form of konbu, kelp, and flakes of bonito, a fish related to tuna. Dashi is essential to Japanese cuisine, but it can be used in many Western dishes too. Both konbu and bonito flakes are readily available in Asian foodstores.

Place the konbu and bonito in cold water and heat slowly; do not let the water come to the boil. Simmer for about 20 minutes, skimming off any foam that might appear, then turn off the heat and let the flakes settle. Strain the liquid through a fine sieve. Use immediately, or cool to room temperature and store, covered, in the refrigerator for up to 4 days.

The Japanese usually make more than one dashi from the same ingredients, soaking the konbu two or even three times, and adding a few fresh bonito flakes. The first dashi has the best flavour and is used for fine or light soups and dishes, while the subsequent dashi are used in dishes with stronger ingredients.

Broccoli Soup

1 small head of broccoli	
2 garlic cloves	
1 small onion	
150 ml (5 fl oz) cream	
olive oil	

Broccoli Soup

It is possible to cook something without adding salt during the process. But chances are that salt *will* have to be added somewhere. There are many ways to illustrate the truth of this, but this soup provides perhaps the best example.

Finely chop the onion and the garlic and sweat in the oil for 5 minutes without colouring. Separate the broccoli into florets and chop the stem into small pieces. Add it to the onion and garlic and pour over enough water to cover by 2 cm (¾ in). Cover and cook over a medium heat for 10 minutes. Transfer to a food processor and blend until smooth. Return to the pot and stir in the cream. Now taste the soup.

It will be tasteless, bland and unappetising. But this is easily remedied. Take a good pinch of sea salt and stir it into the soup. Taste again; there will be an improvement, though less than you will expect. Add another large pinch of salt and taste again. It will be better still. At least a third pinch will be necessary. Taste again, and if the soup is still not to your liking, add another pinch, much smaller this time. That should be enough.

If there is one essential skill in cooking, it is the ability to salt whilst cooking. It is a skill that can only be learned by doing; no recipe can tell you whether something is too salty. You simply have to taste it.

Brine

Salt will always get in, eventually: osmosis means that any solution of varying concentrations, separated by a semi-permeable membrane, will seek to become the same on either side of that membrane. A cell that is saltier but drier than the salt water it is immersed in will, over time, become less salty but more moist. And vice versa.

The simplest brine is of course salt water, at around 3–5% solution, which is strong enough to penetrate most meat, making it moister and more flavourful. The brine should always be poured directly into a nonreactive (glass, plastic, enamel, earthenware) container and left to cool completely before use.

Combine the salt and the water and heat so the salt is thoroughly dissolved, then leave to cool. The brine can be tested by placing an uncooked egg in it; if the egg floats, the brine is strong enough for both curing and flavouring. If the egg sinks, add more salt.

The salt that enters the cells affects both the collagen, or muscle fibres, and the actomyosin, the proteins in muscle tissue, and when heat is applied during cooking the texture of these changes, and the meat becomes juicier and more tender. This alone will improve its flavour. But if it's flavour you're after, there is no need to stop at just salt.

Flavoured Brine

In another of modern life's great ironies, the technologies of food production have resulted in produce which is often less flavourful—the modern pig is up to 50% leaner than its historical counterpart. It means that if you cook pork loin at home, you will often end up with meat that is hard, dry and very lean.

The solution? Brining for flavour.

Because there is more salt in the brine than in the meat, the muscle absorbs the salt water. There, the salt denatures the meat proteins, causing them to unwind and form a matrix that traps the water. And if the brine includes herbs, garlic, juniper berries or peppercorns, those flavours are trapped in the meat, too. Instead of seasoning on the surface only, as most cooks do, brining carries the seasonings throughout.

This is a basic flavoured brine that is good for just about everything. The flavours it imparts are generally subtle, and the sugar both complements and counteracts the salt.

Flavoured Brine #1

600 g (1¼ lb) sea salt	
400 g (14 oz) sugar	
12 each of juniper berries, cloves and black peppercorns	
3 bay leaves	
4 l (8½ pints) water	

Combine all the ingredients in a large pot, cover, and bring to a boil. Boil for 1 minute, stirring to dissolve the salt and sugar. Remove from heat and cool completely before using.

The addition of garlic, herbs and lemon zest means this brine imparts a little more complexity of flavour. Note that there is more water specified for this recipe than for previous brine; this is to carry the greater amount of solid ingredients.

Flavoured Brine #2

290 g (10¼ oz) sea salt	
90 ml (3 fl oz) honey	
12 bay leaves	
35 g (1¼ oz) garlic cloves, skin left on, smashed	
2 tablespoons black peppercorns	
3 large sprigs rosemary	
1 large bunch thyme	
1 large bunch Italian parsley	
zest and juice of 2 large lemons	
4.5 l (9½ pints) water	

Combine all the ingredients in a large pot, cover, and bring to a boil. Boil for 1 minute, stirring to dissolve the salt and honey. Remove from heat and cool completely before using.

Recipes for using flavoured brine can be found on pages 82, 99 and 101.

Oil

In cooking, oil is almost as important as salt. Like salt, oil comes in a variety of types, each with a specific use: fruity single-pressing extra-virgin olive oil to use as a condiment, sesame oil for a unique flavour or vegetable oil for deep-frying.

As with salt, it is best to keep a variety of these oils in your cupboard. And, if you add some good sea salt to a general purpose extra-virgin olive oil and keep it in the fridge, you will have on hand something that is perfect for smearing onto meat before frying, or brushing over vegetables to be baked, or thinned with lemon juice to use as a dressing. Also, the salt will not dissolve in the oil, so you will still be able to see exactly how much you are using.

Salty Oil

2 tablespoons sea salt

extra-virgin olive oil

Put the salt in a small jar and, stirring with a fork, pour in enough olive oil to cover the salt by about 1 cm (⅜ in). Cover with a lid and keep in the refrigerator. The salt will settle to the bottom. When using, either shake the jar to get equal parts salt and oil, or use a spoon to take out the concentration you require.

This oil adds a subtly delicious smoky taste to all that it touches. It is particularly good used as a base for vinaigrette.

Smoked Chilli Salt Oil

2 tablespoons smoked chilli salt (see page 44)

extra-virgin olive oil

Put the salt in a small jar and, stirring with a fork, pour in enough oil to cover the salt by about 1 cm (⅜ in). Cover with a lid and refrigerate.

You can go one step further, and add one of cooking's essential flavours to the mix.

Garlic / Salt / Oil

2 tablespoons sea salt

extra-virgin olive oil

3–4 garlic cloves

Finely chop the garlic cloves. Put them with the salt in a small jar and, stirring with a fork, pour in enough olive oil to cover the salt by about 1 cm (⅜ in). Cover with a lid and refrigerate.

Another useful condiment is anchovy oil. Save the oil in which anchovies have been packed, and filter it through a sieve lined with paper towels. After a while you will amass a good quantity which can be used for frying, seasoning and as a base for sauces and vinaigrettes.

opposite Home-cured gravlax
(see recipe on page 66).

Preserved

For millennia salting, in its various forms, has been mankind's primary method of food preservation. Until the twentieth century. Then, with the advent of refrigeration, the need for salt as a preservative fell away. Coupled with the rise of chemical preservatives, it means the modern household rarely uses the traditional methods of preserving food.

But the arts of curing, fermenting, canning and drying food are too important to be lost. What's more, they are profoundly satisfying to practise. And they produce results which are often superior to those cured foods that are produced on a commercial scale: the first mouthful of your own home-cured ham or beef will soon illustrate that point.

In the following section are guidelines for some basic preserved foods. These are just the beginning. But a word of warning—once you have made your own, you'll possibly never go back!

Cured Wagyu Beef

2 kg (4½ lb) Wagyu strip loin, marble score of 6–7
1 kg (2¼ lb) Murray River washed natural salt
1 kg (2¼ lb) white sugar
50 g (1¾ oz) cracked pink pepper
50 g (1¾ oz) cracked black pepper
rosemary sprigs

Cured Wagyu Beef

Beef is one of the easiest and safest things to cure, and Wagyu will give you the most delicious results. This recipe is from Jason Palmero, Executive Sous Chef at Kobe Jones in Sydney, Australia.

Mix together the salt and the sugar. Layer a few sprigs of rosemary in the bottom of a plastic container large enough to fit the beef. Cover it with some of the salt and sugar mix and lay the beef on top. Use the rest of the salt and sugar mix to cover the fillet, making more (to the same ratio of 40/60) if you don't have enough. Cover the container and put it in the fridge.

After 3 days, remove the beef and rinse it under cold running water. Pat it dry, and then rub the fillet with a good handful of cracked black pepper to remove any remaining moisture. Wrap the fillet in cling film and keep in the refrigerator; as the curing period is relatively brief, the meat should be kept refrigerated and used within a week.

The basic cure can be adjusted with different flavourings: try it with garlic, star anise or rosemary. Once your beef is cured, probably the first thing you'll want to do is put it in a sandwich. And if you use the bread you made from the recipe on page 79, the butter from page 140 and the pickles from page 69, there is a pretty good chance that it will be the best sandwich you ever ate. Why? Because you made it all yourself.

Biltong

Biltong
1 beef silverside
rock salt
cider or white wine vinegar
cracked black pepper
coriander (cilantro) seeds

Biltong

If the reason you are curing food is *preservation*, then you want something that will last a *long* time. Biltong, like its American cousin, jerky, gives you the best of both worlds: it tastes delicious, and it is virtually indestructible.

Cutting along the grain, slice the beef into strips approximately 1 cm (⅜ in) thick by 15 cm (6 in) long. Trim away any excess fat, then sprinkle both sides with a generous amount of rock salt. Leave for at least an hour.

Put some cider vinegar or white wine vinegar in a bowl. Scrape the excess salt from the beef and dip it into the vinegar, shaking off the excess. Sprinkle liberally with pepper and coriander (cilantro) seeds.

The meat is now ready to dry. This may be done outdoors by hanging the strips on a line on a warm, breezy day; cover the meat with a piece of muslin to protect it. Alternatively, hang it in a cool, dry place with a fan going nearby. Drying should not be attempted when the air is humid, otherwise the meat may spoil.

The biltong should be ready in 3 or 4 days. Refrigerate it, or store it lightly wrapped in a cool, airy place, and eat within 6 months.

❧

The above process can be applied to almost any lean meat—the original jerky was made by the Incas from salted alpaca meat. Kangaroo, ostrich and venison are all satisfying substitutes for beef.

5 kg (11 lb) pork belly
sea salt

Salt Pork

Salt pork is similar to biltong in that it will keep virtually forever, but its uses are more varied: diced salt pork can be added to many dishes, bringing to them an added depth of flavour. It also makes a delicious gravy, the recipe for which is on page 121.

The best container for salting pork is a lidded wooden box, such as those used to pack expensive wine. It is useful, too, if there are some small holes through which the juices can escape.

Cut the pork belly into five even pieces. Remove any bones and with a sharp knife make regular incisions in the skin. Cover the bottom of the box with salt, then layer the pork on top, covering with more salt. Work the salt into the pork with your fingers. Add another layer of pork, repeating the process, until all of the pork is covered with salt. Put the lid on the box and leave in a cool place for 4 weeks, with a container underneath to catch the juices.

It is essential that the pork remains well covered with salt, so check the box every few days, and add more salt if necessary. After 4 weeks, remove the pork from the box and wipe it with a cloth. It can now be hung, wrapped in muslin or inside a paper bag, in a cool, dark, well-ventilated place.

Salt pork will last virtually forever; however it will keep getting harder with time. This can be prevented by transferring it to an airtight container and putting it in the fridge after a month or two. If the pork is very hard, or if the taste is too salty, it may be soaked before use.

The above method is adapted from *Preserved* by Nick Sandler and Johnny Acton. This informative book contains detailed instructions for all manner of preservation techniques, and is highly recommended for anyone who is interested in preserving food.

2–3 kg (4½–6½ lb) coarse salt
900 g (2 lb) sugar
1 teaspoon saltpetre (saltpeter)
1 fresh ham, skin on
½ bottle red wine
100 ml (3½ fl oz) balsamic vinegar
55 g (1⅞ oz) fresh pork fat
1 large head of garlic
1 tablespoon cracked black pepper

Sweet-cured Ham

There are many who consider making ham to be the pinnacle of the curing art. Certainly, there are many for whom the satisfaction of slicing into their first home-cured ham proves to be one of life's culinary high points. Second only to *eating* the ham, of course.

Weigh the ham. Make a sweet-cure by combining the salt, sugar and saltpetre (saltpeter). Rub it vigorously into the ham, especially around the bone. Put the ham in a wooden box and cover with a cloth. The ham needs to cure in a cool place for 5 days per kilo (2¼ lb) of meat. Check it regularly to ensure that it remains well covered with the curing mix, and add more if necessary.

At the end of the curing period, remove the ham from the box and rinse it thoroughly with water. Dry it with a cloth. Boil the wine and balsamic vinegar together until they have reduced by half, and use this liquid to wash the ham all over. Tie a strong cord around the shank and hang the ham in a cool, well-ventilated place for 24 hours.

Mince the garlic in a food processor and mix it with the pork fat, pepper and a tablespoon of salt. Rub this paste all over the ham, then wrap the ham in a piece of muslin and put it inside a large paper bag which should form a loose shroud. Hang in the same cool, well-ventilated place.

The ham will be ready in around 3 months. Ensure that it remains dry, and it will keep for at least 6 months. Use a long, sharp knife to slice what you need, then return the ham to its wrapping.

Like the previous recipe, this recipe is also adapted from one featured in *Preserved*.

Gravlax

1 salmon fillet, skin on
for each kg (2¼ lb) of salmon:
50 g (1¾ oz) sea salt
50 g (1¾ oz) sugar
½ teaspoon cracked black pepper
zest of 2 lemons
50 g (1¾ oz) fresh dill

Gravlax

If the idea of making ham seems like too much of a commitment, gravlax is the perfect compromise. And unlike the Scandinavian fishermen who invented it in the Middle Ages, there is no need to make your gravlax by burying your fish in the sand above the high tide line; it will taste fantastic after just two days in the refrigerator.

Mix all the curing ingredients together in a bowl. Trim the salmon and remove any pin bones. Place it in a shallow dish, skin side down, and rub the cure into the flesh. Cover the salmon with a layer of cling film and place a chopping board on top, weighted down with two or three cans.

Put the salmon in the refrigerator. After 24 hours, drain off any excess liquid, turn the salmon over and weight it down again. After a further 24 hours, the gravlax will be ready.

If left whole, the gravlax will keep for another five days. When you are ready to serve it, use a long, sharp knife to slice the flesh on the diagonal, starting at the tail end.

If you wish to spice up your gravlax a little, sprinkle a shot glass worth of vodka or pastis over the salmon, then refrigerate for an hour before applying the curing mixture.

Garlic Sausages

Garlic Sausages
1 kg (2¼ lb) pork shoulder
300 g (10½ oz) hard pork back fat
35 g (1¼ oz) salt
5 garlic cloves
1 teaspoon cracked black pepper
1 teaspoon herbes salées
½ teaspoon cayenne pepper
¼ teaspoon nutmeg
30 ml (1 fl oz) brandy
¼ teaspoon acidophilus powder
¼ teaspoon saltpetre (saltpeter)
sausage casings

Garlic Sausages

Like cheese and pickled vegetables, sausages are among the very oldest of food preparation methods. Basically, sausages fall into four categories: cooked, smoked, raw and dried. Dried sausages, such as this garlic sausage, are cured by lactic acid fermentation, which is kicked off by the acidophilus powder, and are eaten raw.

Half an hour or so before grinding, place the meat in the freezer; it should chill almost to the point of freezing. Keeping the meat thoroughly chilled is essential—if it warms, the protein and fats in the sausage can separate, causing the sausage to break when it cooks, resulting in a coarse, grainy texture. It's also a good idea to chill the grinder and stuffer attachments before using.

Mince the pork shoulder with a "medium" disc on the mincer. Cut the pork fat into strips about 20 x 5 mm (¾ x ¼ in). Place all the ingredients in a bowl and mix together thoroughly.

Prepare the casings by soaking them in cold water for a few minutes. Drain the water and refill. Making sure your sink is clean, put about 10 cm (4 in) of water into it and transfer the casings. Flush each one by filling with water from the top.

Once cleaned, put them back in the bowl of fresh water, only taking them out as you are prepared to stuff them.

Stuff the casings, making sausages that are about 25 cm (9¾ in) long, and tie up the ends. Hang the garlic sausages in a warm place for 48 hours, then transfer to a cool place to hang. To avoid contamination, make sure no sausage touches another. The temperature should be a constant 15°C (59°F), and after about the fifth day the sausages will bloom with a white mould. It is perfectly normal, being a product of the lactic acid produced by fermentation.

The sausages should hang for at least 4 months, but will be better after 6 months.

Herbes Salées

As herbs can be used to flavour salt, so salt can be used to preserve herbs. *Herbes salées*, salted herbs, is a classic French preparation. The convenience of this mixture makes it invaluable. Use for soups, stews, marinades, in sauces or indeed anywhere.

Herbes Salées

25 g (⅞ oz) chives, chopped	
25 g (⅞ oz) savory, chopped	
25 g (⅞ oz) parsley, chopped	
25 g (⅞ oz) chervil, chopped	
90 g (3 oz) spring onions (scallions), chopped	
25 g (⅞ oz) celery leaves, chopped	
140 g (5 oz) carrots, grated	
145 g (5⅛ oz) sea salt	

Combine all the herbs together in a bowl. In a crock or glass bowl, place a thick layer of the herb mixture and sprinkle generously with salt. Repeat until all the herb mixture is used, cover and refrigerate for 2 weeks. Drain off the accumulated liquid. Pack the herb mixture into sterilised jars and refrigerate until ready to use.

Salting herbs is the perfect introduction to salt's preservative magic. The same basic process applies to almost any type of food, from ham to cabbage, cherries to cod: the salt draws moisture from the food, making it less hospitable for any bacteria, and at the same time acts as an antibacterial agent itself. It also serves to flavour the food it is curing, thereby providing three benefits in one.

Preserved Lemons

Preserved lemons are one of the defining flavours of North African cuisine —a chicken *tagine* without preserved lemons is unthinkable—but their use extends far beyond that. In fact, preserved lemons can be used in any dish that needs a salty, citrus *zing* to lift it above the ordinary.

Preserved Lemons

10–12 lemons	
sea salt	
4 bay leaves	
6 cloves	
1 teaspoon peppercorns	
1 teaspoon coriander (cilantro) seeds	
1 500 ml (17 fl oz) preserving jar, sterilised	

Choose unwaxed lemons, and wash and rinse them thoroughly. One at a time, cut the lemons into quarters from the base to the stem, but not cutting all the way through. Fill the cavity thoroughly with salt, a clove and a few of the peppercorns and coriander (cilantro) seeds. Pack the lemons into the jar along with the bay leaves until there is about 3 cm (1 in) of space at the top of the jar.

Juice the remaining lemons and pour the juice into the jar. If there is not enough to cover the lemons, top up with water. Seal the jar and leave in a cool, dark place for at least 1 month, inverting the jars occasionally to distribute the brine. The lemons will keep for about a year.

Dill Pickles

Pickles are generally made with vinegar—its active ingredient, acetic acid, inhibits the growth of microbes and therefore prevents spoilage. But salt has a very active part to play. Below is a simple recipe for dill pickles, but you can use the same basic process to pickle just about anything.

Dill Pickles

6 large pickling cucumbers
125 g (4½ oz) sea salt
300 ml (10 fl oz) cider vinegar
1.8 l (3⅜ pints) water
2 sprigs of dill
4 cardamom pods
6 cloves
12 peppercorns
2 x 800 ml (1¾ pint) preserving jar, sterilised

Slice the cucumbers lengthways and deseed them. Make a pickling brine by heating the water to boiling point and stirring in the salt until it has dissolved. Leave to cool, then add the vinegar.

Sterilise the jars, then pack the sliced cucumber, distributing the dill, cardamom, cloves and peppercorns among them. Pour over the cooled brine and then seal. Leave in the refrigerator for at least 1 month before using.

Pickling really is that simple, and using the same basic concept, you can now pickle anything you choose, from onions to walnuts, quails eggs to peppers. Even octopus, if you're feeling adventurous!

Olives

Of course, no one *needs* to cure their own olives, but that's really no reason not to. Like making pickles, preserving lemons or curing meat, it is relatively simple, yet provides great satisfaction.

Olives

2.5 kg (5½ lb) mature green olives
3 tablespoons salt
2 lemons
2 tablespoons dried oregano
500 ml (17 fl oz) white wine vinegar
6 garlic cloves
2 tablespoons cumin seeds, crushed
olive oil

Hit each olive with something heavy—a rolling pin or a hammer—to crack the flesh. Rinse with cold water. Put the olives in a nonreactive container and cover with cold water. Weigh them down and keep them in a cool, dark place for 10 days, changing the water every day.

Make a brine from the salt and 1.5 l (3¼ pints) of water. Rinse the olives in cold water and then cover them with the brine. Cut the lemons into small cubes, cut the garlic cloves in half add them to the brine with the oregano, vinegar and cumin. Float enough olive oil on top to cover the surface. Store in a cool, dark place for at least 2 weeks, by which time the olives should be ready.

Sauerkraut

2 large, fresh cabbages
sea salt

Sauerkraut

Sauerkraut, it must be noted, is an acquired taste. But once you have acquired it, you can never get enough.

Remove the outer leaves and the core from the cabbages and cut them into quarters. Finely shred the cabbage using a food processor or a large, sharp knife.

Sterilise a large, nonreactive container by pouring boiling water down the sides and letting it sit for 5 minutes. Weigh the shredded cabbage; you will need 2 heaped tablespoons of salt per kilo (2¼ lb) of cabbage. Empty the water from the fermenting container, add the salt and the cabbage and mix it thoroughly.

The salt will soon begin to draw the juices from the cabbage. With your hands, gently press the cabbage into the container so that the brine rises to the surface; in order to ferment, the cabbage must stay immersed at all time. The best way to ensure this happens is by covering the cabbage with a plate that is almost the same size as the mouth of your container. Make a brine of 1¼ tablespoons of salt per litre (2⅛ pints) of water, and use this to fill a large plastic bag. This will weigh down the plate, and if it leaks a little the cabbage will not be watered down.

Cover the container with plastic wrap or a heavy cloth. For best results, the cabbage should be stored in a dark place with an ambient temperature of 18°C (64°F) and left to ferment for 5–6 weeks. When the sauerkraut is ready, transfer it into sterilised jars and seal. It will keep in the refrigerator for up to 6 months.

Sauerkraut may be eaten either raw or cooked. Many remarkable health benefits have been ascribed to the regular consumption of raw sauerkraut, but it is not for everybody. To cook sauerkraut, drain it and rinse in cold running water first. Place it in an ovenproof dish and moisten with a little white wine or some stock and whatever seasonings you like, then cook at 180°C (355°F).

Kimchi

1 kg (2¼ lb) bok choi	
salt	
3 garlic cloves	
2 teaspoons ginger, chopped	
3 red chillies	
1 bunch spring onions (scallions)	
2 teaspoons sugar	
2 tablespoons fish sauce	
1 tablespoon soy sauce	
1.4 l (3 pints) water	

Kimchi

It's easy to think of kimchi as "Asian sauerkraut", but they are in fact quite different. Kimchi may be prepared from many vegetables other than cabbage, depending on where it is being made, although *baechu* (cabbage) kimchi is still the most common. This version is made with bok choi, and is well spiced. After you have mastered the basics, the world of kimchi available to you is almost infinite.

Wash the bok choi thoroughly, then chop roughly and put into a large bowl. Dissolve 3 tablespoons of salt into 750 ml (1½ pint) of water and pour over the bok choi. Cover the leaves with a plate, ensure everything is fully immersed in the brine, and leave for 8 hours. Drain off the brine, soak the leaves for 10 minutes in cold, fresh water, and drain this too.

Finely chop the garlic, chillies and spring onions (scallions) and add them with the rest of the ingredients to a brine made of 1½ tablespoons of salt dissolved in 650 ml (1⅜ pint) of water. Place the bok choi in a large sterilised glass jar and pour the brine over them, again ensuring all the leaves are covered. Seal the jar and leave in a warm place (above 24°C [75°F]) for 24 hours before refrigerating. The kimchi will last about a month.

opposite Many cocktails are enhanced by the addition of a flavoured salt around the rim of the glass; serve with prosciutto and melon balls for the perfect salty snack (see recipes on page 74).

Most Appetising

Astounding as it may seem, during the 1800s it was common for American saloons to have bowls of caviar sitting on their bar tops for patrons to dip in to, thereby increasing their thirst for beer. Of course, caviar was a lot less exclusive in the nineteenth century—indeed, sturgeon could still be found swimming in New York's Hudson River.

The practice of giving away salty food continues today, only the caviar has been replaced by less expensive items, such as pretzels and salted nuts. But the intent is the same—if your customers are offered free salty snacks, they will drink more.

These days, drinking *more* is not the point. But small, salty appetisers are still an ideal way to accompany drinks, or to begin a meal. Always buy the best quality produce you can find. Combine ingredients in a way that ensures tastes complement each other. Keep things simple. And enjoy...

Margarita

Many say that a classic cocktail cannot be improved upon. In this case, the addition of a little homemade smoked chilli salt might be the exception to the rule.

Margarita

3 lime wedges
smoked chilli salt
75 ml (2½ fl oz) tequila
80 ml (2¾ fl oz) lime juice
25 ml (⅞ fl oz) Cointreau
ice

Rub the rims of two glasses with a wedge of lime, then dip them into the chilli salt. Shake the tequila, lime juice and Cointreau together in a cocktail shaker with ice. Strain into a cocktail glass and garnish with a wedge of lime.

Melon and Prosciutto

A classic combination. The melon should be ripe but not soft, the prosciutto should be sliced paper thin, and the sweet, salty contrast should be heavenly.

Melon and Prosciutto

1 ripe rockmelon (canteloupe) or honeydew melon
6 slices prosciutto
Persian blue or other finishing salt

Using a melon baller, scoop out the flesh of the melon. Slice the prosciutto into small strips, slightly larger than the circumference of the melon balls. Wrap the prosciutto around the melon and secure with a toothpick. Lay the melon balls on their side and sprinkle each with an attractive finishing salt such as Persian blue salt.

Parmesan

It's easy to think of parmesan as something you only grate over pasta. But nothing could be further from the truth. *Parmigiano-Reggiano* is one of the world's great cheeses, and nothing makes this more apparent than when it is eaten by itself, giving you a chance to savour its salty, nutty flavour and unique texture. And if you combine it with melon and prosciutto and a margarita it's, well...

Parmesan

aged Parmigiano-Reggiano

Buy the best quality Parmigiano-Reggiano you can find, preferably one which is stravecchio or very old, having been aged for at least 3 years. Break into small pieces and serve with the margarita and the melon and prosciutto.

Caviar

On second thought, perhaps *this* is the perfect appetiser.

Caviar

caviar

rye bread

unsalted butter

sour cream

vodka

Buy the very best caviar you can afford: you may only do this once in your life. If the caviar has been in the refrigerator, take it out at least an hour before you will eat it. Lightly toast some thin slices of rye bread and butter it sparingly. Put spoonfuls of caviar on the hot toast and top with a small amount of sour cream. Follow the caviar with a sip of chilled vodka.

Spanish Almonds

In the end, food is a matter of personal taste. Certainly caviar doesn't appeal to everyone. Salted nuts, on the other hand, are almost universal.

Spanish Almonds

450 g (16 oz) raw almonds
2 teaspoons cumin
1 teaspoon smoked paprika
1 teaspoon dried thyme
¼ teaspoon cayenne pepper
45 g (1½ oz) light brown sugar
1 tablespoon sea salt
1 egg white

Place all of the dry ingredients in a large bowl and stir to combine. Whisk the egg white with a tablespoon of water until it is foamy. Pour over the almonds and stir to coat; strain to remove excess and transfer to the bowl of spices. Stir well.

Preheat the oven to 130°C (265°F). Transfer the nuts to a rimmed baking tray lightly greased with oil. Bake the almonds for 30 minutes. Shake the baking tray, reduce the heat to 110°C (230°F) and bake until the almonds are dry and golden, about another 30 minutes. Serve while still warm.

Salt Crackers

It might seem that, with a limitless variety of crackers available from the supermarket, there is no need to make your own. But as these salt crackers are so delicious, and take little more than 20 minutes to make, there really is no reason not to. After all, everybody loves crackers.

Salt Crackers

1.125 kg (2½ lb) strong white flour
2 teaspoons baking powder
1 teaspoon poppy seeds
1 teaspoon dill seeds
1 teaspoon caraway seeds
2 teaspoons table salt
175 ml (6 fl oz) extra-virgin olive oil
around 400 ml (13½ fl oz) cold water

Sift together the flour and baking powder then add the rest of the dry ingredients. Stir in the olive oil, then very slowly add the water, stopping before the dough becomes sticky.

Dust the work surface and a rolling pin with flour and roll the dough out to a thickness of about 5 mm (¼ in). Cut into the desired shape. Roll the cut shapes further so they are very flat, and transfer to a baking tray. Sprinkle with sea salt and bake at 200°C (390°F) for about 10 minutes or until golden: they will need to be watched carefully to avoid burning.

Soft Pretzels

Soft Pretzels
375 ml (12¾ fl oz) warm water
1 tablespoon sugar
2 teaspoons table salt
1 packet active dried yeast
675 g (1½ lb) cups plain (all-purpose) flour
50 g (1¾ oz) unsalted butter
vegetable oil
2.5 l (5¼ pints) water
150 g (5¼ oz) baking soda
1 egg yolk
sea salt for sprinkling

Soft Pretzels

The shape of the pretzel is claimed to represent that of praying hands. Certainly there is a long European tradition of pretzels being eaten on religious occasions. The tradition of pretzels being eaten whilst drinking beer is probably just as old.

Use a mixer with a dough hook. Combine the water, sugar and salt in the mixing bowl. Sprinkle the yeast on top. Sit for 5 minutes until the mixture begins to foam. Mix on low speed while adding the flour and butter, then increase the speed and knead until the dough is smooth and pulls away from the side of the bowl. Remove the dough, clean the bowl and oil it lightly. Return the dough to the bowl, cover with cling film and sit in a warm place until the dough has doubled in size; it will take about 1 hour.

Cover two baking trays with baking paper and oil lightly. Heat the oven to 230°C (445°F). Bring the water and the baking soda to the boil in a large saucepan or roasting pan. In a small bowl, whisk the egg yolk with a tablespoon of water.

Turn the dough on to a lightly oiled surface and divide in eight equal pieces. Roll out each piece of dough into a rope about 60 cm (23½ in) long. Make a "U" shape with the dough, cross the ends over and bring back down, pressing them on to the bottom of the "U" to make a pretzel shape.

Put the pretzels, one by one, into the boiling water for 30 seconds, then place them on the baking tray. Brush the top of each pretzel with the egg and sprinkle generously with sea salt. Bake for up to 15 minutes, until the pretzels are a dark, golden brown. Remove them from the oven and let the pretzels cool on a rack before serving.

Focaccia with Olive and Rosemary

400 g (14 oz) "00" bread flour
2 teaspoons instant dried yeast
2 teaspoons table salt
250 ml (8½ oz) warm water
3 tablespoons olive oil
75 g (2½ oz) pitted black olives
fresh rosemary
coarse sea salt for sprinkling

Focaccia with Olive and Rosemary

Focaccia is extremely quick and easy to make. The dough is also perfect for making pizza bases.

Place the yeast, flour and salt in the bowl of an electric mixer with a dough hook and mix at low speed, gradually adding the water and the olive oil. Mix for 5–7 minutes until the dough is smooth. This process may be done by hand, but will take about twice as long.

Place the dough in a lightly oiled bowl, cover with cling film and set aside in a warm place until it has doubled in size. Gently knock back the dough with a fist to remove the air, then knead by hand for a few minutes. Divide into two pieces and place on baking trays. Flatten the dough into ovals and use your fingers to make indents in the top. Gently press olives into the indentations and scatter over small sprigs of rosemary.

Let the dough rest for 5–10 minutes. Meanwhile, preheat the oven to 200°C (390°F). Sprinkle the focaccia with a generous amount of sea salt and bake until golden, approximately 15 minutes. Best eaten while still warm.

White Bread

15 g (½ oz) fresh yeast	
400 ml (13½ fl oz) warm water	
675 g (1½ lb) strong white flour	
2 teaspoons table salt	
1 tablespoon butter	

White Bread

Salt plays a vital role in bread making. If there is too little of it, the interior of the loaf will not open up, becoming dense and stodgy. You will need to experiment; different combination of flour, yeast and salt will provide different results. But if you use the basic recipe below, after a few loaves you will get to know how the ingredients work together, and your bread will be perfect every time.

Blend the yeast with a little of the warm water, then add the rest of the water to thin the paste to a milky consistency. Cover and leave in a warm place until frothy.

Mix the flour and the salt and then rub in the butter. Add the yeast liquid to the dry ingredients and mix to form a firm dough, adding more flour if it is too sticky. Turn the dough on to a lightly floured work surface and knead until firm and elastic. Shape the dough into a ball and place it inside a lightly oiled plastic bag. Leave to rise in a warm place.

When the dough has doubled in size, remove from the plastic bag and knock the dough back before shaping into one large or two small loaves. Cover with a cloth and leave to rise until doubled in size. Bake in an oven that has been preheated to 200°C (390°F) for about 40 minutes for a large loaf or 30-35 minutes for small loaves. 10 minutes into the baking time, spray the loaves in the oven with water using a plastic atomizer bottle: this will improve the crust. The bread is done when, if you tap the bottom of the loaf, it sounds hollow.

From the Sea

Cooking fish and seafood correctly is a sensitive art; the flesh is often delicate, as are the flavours, and tastes and textures need to be enhanced, not overpowered. At the same time, it's possible that fish and seafood can be cooked in more ways than any other type of protein.

The art lies in the cooking method, timing and in seasoning. A fresh, plump oyster, for example, benefits from no cooking and very little seasoning. A fresh scallop needs just the barest acquaintance with heat and a few well-chosen flavourings to bring out its best. Salmon fillets are equally good cured or cooked. And a whole fish benefits greatly from being baked in some type of parcel, so that none of its essential moisture escapes.

Salt brings something to all of these processes, as the following pages will show. But it is in seasoning fish and seafood that salt can shine brightest. The salting of seafood must be done skilfully, but with imagination. Flavoured salts can work wonders: a hint of coffee or vanilla, citrus or fennel will raise a dish out of the ordinary.

As always, there are so many possibilities, so experiment, taste, enjoy.

Brined Trout

| flavoured brine #1 (recipe page 58) |
| 1 garlic clove, crushed |
| 2 medium trout, filleted, with skin on |

Brined Trout

The danger with cooking any type of fish lies in overcooking, letting the delicate flesh dry out and become rubbery and tasteless. Brining the fillets, however, allows them to be cooked at a greater heat, giving the outside a crisp, salty crust, while leaving the flesh beneath moist and tender, particularly when grilled.

Make up one-quarter portion of the flavoured brine from page 58, with the addition of 1 crushed garlic clove. Lay the trout fillets in a shallow glass dish and pour the brine over them. Refrigerate for 2 hours. Remove the fillets from the brine and cook under a hot grill, skin side up, for 4 minutes, then turn over and cook for a further 4 minutes.

This recipe will work for any firm, white-fleshed fish—just be sure to leave the skin on the fillets so that they hold together during cooking. The fish should need no further sauce or seasoning, other than a squeeze of lemon juice and a little cracked black pepper.

Whole Fish Baked in Salt

1 whole fish, about 1 kg (2¼ lb), with head, tail, and scales left on

10 whole Tellicherry peppercorns

4 bay leaves

1 kg (2¼ lb) coarse sea salt

extra-virgin olive oil

chervil

Whole Fish Baked in Salt

Baking is possibly the easiest way in which to cook fish—you don't even need to remove the scales. Simply cover, cook and then clean off the salt. Both the skin and the scales will come off with the salt, leaving you with moist, tender, perfectly-cooked flesh.

Rinse the fish with cold water, pat it dry and refrigerate until just before cooking.

Pour a good layer of salt in the bottom of an ovenproof baking dish that is just larger than the fish. Lay 2 bay leaves on the salt, then place the fish on the leaves. Place the peppercorns inside the cavity of the fish, then top with the other 2 bay leaves. Pour the remaining salt over the fish to cover it, leaving the tail fin exposed, if necessary.

Place the fish on the middle rack in the centre of the oven and bake for 25 minutes at 200°C (390°F). Remove the fish from the oven and gently crack off the layer of salt: most of the skin will come off with the salt. Drizzle with olive oil and garnish with chervil.

—

Unfortunately, using this method means you cannot check the fish while it is cooking. However, because the salt crust seals in the moisture, it is unlikely that the fish will overcook. If in doubt, take the fish from the oven a little earlier than you normally would; the salt will also trap the heat, so the fish will continue cooking until you break the crust open.

Fish Fillets Baked in Salt

6 white fish fillets
1½–2 kg (3¾–4½ lb) coarse sea salt
2 egg whites
2 lemons, thinly sliced
1 bunch flat-leaf parsley
125 ml (4¼ fl oz) water

Fish Fillets Baked in Salt

If your fish is already filleted, you can still bake it in salt, you just need to be a little more careful when removing the crust, so that the fillets remain in one piece. Binding the salt with egg whites helps with this process.

In a large bowl, mix together the salt, egg whites and the water. It will result in a loose, sticky paste. Spread a layer of this salt paste on a baking tray and lay the lemon slices on top. Place the fish on top of the lemons, then cover it with the parsley. Top the fish with the remainder of the salt paste.

Bake the fish in the oven at 200°C (390°F) for 15 minutes, then remove it and let rest for another 5–10 minutes, during which time the fish will continue to cook. Carefully break apart the salt crust and extract the fish fillets before serving.

———

Use this method with large fillets, or with steaks. Again, cook the fish for a little less time than you usually would.

12 green prawns (shrimp), unshelled

rock salt

Prawns (Shrimp) Cooked in Rock Salt

All around the Mediterranean, this is one of the most common ways of preparing seafood. Try it with prawns (shrimp), yabbies, Morton Bay bugs or even small lobsters. Simply adjust the cooking times to suit.

Take two cast iron frying pans of about the same size and pour a thick layer of salt in the bottom of each. Heat both pans over a high heat for 7–8 minutes, until the salt is very hot. Place half of the prawns (shrimp) in one pan, and pour the salt from the other pan on top of them. Cook for 3–4 minutes, then remove the prawns (shrimp) with a set of tongs. Return half the salt to the second pan, allow it to reheat, then repeat with the remaining prawns (shrimp).

You don't strictly need two pans for this process: all of the salt can be heated in the one pan and then shovelled over the prawns after they have been put in. And if you do it that way, this recipe becomes the perfect illustration that a kitchen truly need be nothing more than a pan, a flame, a knife and some salt.

20 raw king prawns (jumbo shrimp), peeled and deveined

10 bay leaves

1 tablespoon sea salt

extra-virgin olive oil

Barbecued Prawns (Shrimp) with Bay Salt

Barbecuing should not be complicated—you don't want convoluted procedures or long lists of ingredients. This is where flavoured salts are ideal. The following recipe, adapted from Jamie Oliver, shows how an unexpected combination of flavours, bay leaves and prawns (shrimp), can be brought together perfectly by the smoky heat of the barbecue. You could also try coconut salt or coffee salt for seafood, or use a rub made from one of the combination salts on page 48 to enliven fish or meat.

Soak five wooden skewers in some cold water for 10 minutes. Thread 5 prawns (shrimp) onto each skewer, make sure you poke through the fat and the thin part of each prawn (shrimp).

Crumble the bay leaves into a mortar and pestle and add the salt. Pound the bay leaf and salt mixture until you have a vibrant green salt and the bay leaves have broken down and released all of their natural oils.

Sprinkle each of the kebabs with a good pinch of the bay salt. Drizzle them with a little olive oil and pat and rub everything in. Place the skewers on the hot barbecue. After 1–2 minutes, turn the skewers over and cook for a further minute.

Another great method of applying salt to fish is the salted lemon. Cut lemons are covered with salt and then wrapped in muslin. When you squeeze the lemon, its juice dissolves the salt, and the salt tempers the harshness of the citrus. The resulting salty, tangy juice combines perfectly with the natural ocean flavours. And it makes a great talking point, too.

Salt and Pepper Squid

1 kg (2¼ lb) squid, including the tentacles

10–20 dried red chillies

3 tablespoons sea salt

2 tablespoons black peppercorns

2 tablespoons Sichuan peppercorns

500 g (1¼ lb) rice flour

500 ml (17 fl oz) peanut oil

3 egg whites

coriander (cilantro)

limes

Salt and Pepper Squid

Salt and pepper are without doubt the world's most common seasonings. Many would say that they reach the peak of their achievements in salt and pepper squid. But this method needn't be confined only to squid: you can make salt and pepper prawns (shrimp), or salt and pepper tofu. In fact, the seasoned rice flour can be used to dust just about anything.

Dry roast the chillies, salt and peppercorns in a heavy frying pan over a medium heat until they become fragrant and the salt takes on a light golden colour. Place in a mortar and leave to cool, then grind to a fine consistency. Remove to a bowl and mix in the rice flour.

Heat the oil in a wok until it reaches 180°C (355°F). Cut the squid into strips, keeping the tentacles whole. Beat the egg whites until they are foamy. Dip the squid pieces briefly in the egg white, shake off any excess, then dust lightly with the seasoned flour. Fry for 3–4 minutes, working in small batches so that the oil remains hot. Drain on absorbent paper, then serve with chopped coriander (cilantro) and lime wedges.

Salt-block Salmon

1 Himalayan salt block
2 fillets of fresh salmon, around 250 g (8¾ oz) each
10 g (⅜ oz) fresh lemon thyme
10 g (⅜ oz) fresh rosemary
10 g (⅜ oz) mandarin zest
10 g (⅜ oz) dried freshly ground fennel seeds
25 ml (⅞ fl oz) olive oil
1 mandarin
1 fennel bulb

Salt-block Salmon

The Himalayan salt block (page 19) is perfect for seafood, and for this recipe the surface of the block is lightly flavoured with fennel seeds. Just remember, the salt block will be very hot, and sometimes the edges may crumble a little, depending on its age, so be very careful.

Chop the lemon thyme, rosemary and mandarin zest and place into a mixing bowl with a generous dash of olive oil, enough to create a paste. Rub the salmon fillets with the spice blend and place onto a clean plate to marinate.

Place the salt block into the preheated oven and slowly raise the temperature to 250°C (480°F). When this temperature is reached, carefully take the block out of the oven.

Sprinkle the dried freshly ground fennel seeds on the salt block. Let the seeds start smoking and slightly change colour—it will take about a minute—then lightly blow off the seeds and place salmon fillets skin side down. Let them cook through for approximately 2 minutes before turning. Let them cook for another 2 minutes or until medium rare—this will depend on heat loss from the salt block. Serve with a squeeze of fresh mandarin juice and very thinly sliced fresh fennel tossed in olive oil.

The salt block is best used for those things that will cook quickly—thin fillets are best to ensure that they cook through before the block loses its heat.

Tuna Carpaccio

Tuna Carpaccio
500 g (1⅛ lb) of sashimi-grade tuna
6 tablespoons of Kewpie (Japanese mayonnaise)
6 teaspoons of sushi vinegar
3 garlic cloves, crushed
sea salt
cracked black pepper
pinch of togarashi (Japanese seven spice)
capers
2 teaspoons powdered wasabi

Tuna Carpaccio

The original beef carpaccio was invented at Harry's bar in Venice in the 1950s, and named for the fifteenth century artist Vittore Carpaccio, who was well-known for his use of bright colours. This version uses tuna, and if made on a Himalayan salt slab, it too can look like a work of art.

Place a plate into the freezer. In a bowl, mix the sushi vinegar and crushed garlic together and let sit for about 30 minutes. Strain the vinegar and mix in the mayonnaise, wasabi and salt.

Put the tuna in the freezer for 10 minutes, then, with a very sharp knife, slice the tuna into thin slices. Remove the plate from freezer and arrange the tuna on it in a symmetrical pattern, making sure the tuna pieces do not touch one another. Place the plate with tuna back into freezer for about 15 minutes.

Remove plate from freezer and drizzle the sauce over the tuna. Dress with cracked pepper and a pinch of togarashi. Top generously with capers.

If you have a Himalayan salt block, this recipe would suit it perfectly: chill the salt block for an hour, then arrange the sliced tuna on it. Dress the carpaccio and serve immediately, otherwise the tuna may become too salty.

Salt-block Scallops

A salt block is particularly suitable for scallops, which require just the barest amount of cooking time. To make it more interesting, carefully transfer the salt block to a trivet in the middle of the table and let your guests cook their own.

Scallops with Vanilla Salt

12 fresh scallops

1 teaspoon ginger, minced

1 garlic clove, minced

lemon juice

olive oil

a knob of unsalted butter

1 Himalayan salt block

In a bowl, mix together the ginger and garlic with a splash of olive oil and a squeeze of lemon. Remove the coral from the scallops (if desired) and place them in the marinade. Slowly heat the salt block by putting it in a cold oven and raising the temperature by 50°C (120°F) every 10 minutes. After 10 minutes at 250°C (480°F), quickly but carefully remove it from the oven and place it on a trivet in the centre of the table.

Put a tablespoon of the marinade and a knob of butter in the middle of the salt block and as soon as the butter begins to foam, add a few of the scallops; leave them to sizzle for 1 minute then turn them with a set of tongs. Leave for another 30 seconds, then swirl them through the butter as you remove them from the salt block. Repeat with the rest of the scallops. Serve on individual plates, seasoned with a small pinch of vanilla salt.

You do not have to heat the salt block to "cook" scallops—freezing it will produce equally delicious results.

Scallop Carpaccio

3 very fresh diver scallops

1 tablespoon champagne vinegar

1 tablespoon honey

3 tablespoons grape seed oil

cracked black pepper

1 Himalayan salt block

Put the scallops in the freezer for 5 minutes, then, using a very sharp paring knife, carefully cut each scallop into four thin slices. Put them on a plate, cover and store in the refrigerator until ready to serve.

Place the vinegar and honey in a small bowl and whisk until well combined. Whisking constantly, gradually incorporate the grape seed oil, drop by drop. Once all the ingredients are well combined, keep whisking until you have the consistency of a light mayonnaise. Season with pepper.

Brush the salt block with some of the vinaigrette mixture. Place the scallop slices on the block and drizzle the rest of the emulsion over the scallops. Serve immediately, but wait for 5 minutes before eating—the scallops will cure before your eyes.

opposite Salt-block scallops and vanilla-salted butter—a perfect match.

opposite Salting your steak in advance (see recipe on page 94) results in more tender, flavourful meat.

The Main Course

What is the perfect steak?

Common sense would tell us there is no such thing; one person's perfect steak is another person's lump of undercooked beef, and indeed, for a vegetarian there exists no such thing.

But there are certain universal qualities that a great steak possesses; everyone can agree that a great steak must be moist, flavourful and tender, irrespective of whether it is served rare or well done.

The same applies to all meat, game and fish. Which is why salt is so useful when it comes to preparing them. Not only in the seasoning—which is fundamental—but also as a method of cooking.

Certainly meat and fish need to be seasoned appropriately. But we find that by immersing a less flavourful cut in brine for a few hours we can dramatically improve its quality. And using salt to make a crust or a dough in which to bake meat or fish serves the double purpose of sealing in the moisture and adding to the flavour.

For the following methods you will need to have on hand a reasonably large quantity of salt. In this regard, it is best to buy rock salt in bulk, as it is the cheapest, and will last for as long as you need it.

The Perfect Steak

Knowing that salt draws moisture from food, this method of preparing steak may seem counterintuitive if we want our meat to be moist and juicy. But work it does, particularly on cheaper cuts which are likely to be a little less tender.

Here's how it works. The salt will draw some of the moisture from the meat; that moisture dissolves some of the salt, and then osmosis draws that salted water back into the meat, in an attempt to even out the quantities of both moisture and salt. When the salt is absorbed into the meat, it begins to denature the protein cells, unwinding their regular structure so that they become like little bird's nests. And when the heat of the cooking begins to liquefy that fat within the muscle and to heat up the moisture within the cells, the proteins trap all of that flavourful goodness within the meat. Which results in…

The Perfect Steak

steak, preferably sirloin
coarse salt
red wine
beef stock
butter
cracked black pepper

You will need to prepare the meat at least 1½ hours before serving. Cover the surface of a plate with salt, and place the steak on top of it. Cover the top surface of the steak with salt so that the meat cannot be seen. Let this stand for an hour.

Heat a heavy cast-iron frying pan so that it is very hot. Meanwhile, brush all of the salt from the steak and pat very dry with paper towels. Pour a little oil into the frying pan and as it heats to smoking point, grind a little fresh black pepper over the steak. Carefully place the steak into the pan and cook without touching for 4 minutes. Turn the steak and cook for another 3 minutes.

Turn down the heat, take the steak from the pan, put it on a plate and cover loosely with foil to rest. Pour a small splash of red wine into the pan and scrape with a spatula to deglaze. Add an equal splash of beef stock and stir whilst reducing. When it is reduced by half, turn off the heat and add a small knob of butter, incorporating it by making gentle waves in the sauce with the spatula.

Transfer the steak to a serving plate, pouring any remaining juices back into the sauce. Add a final twist of black pepper to the sauce and pour over the steak. Serve with a simple green salad.

❧

It is important that you only use coarse sea salt for this recipe, and that the salt is brushed off completely and the steak patted thoroughly dry before cooking, otherwise the finished meat may become too salty.

opposite Accompany your steak and salad with a finishing salt such as Cyprus black (below left) or, for the salad, Cyprus citrus (below right).

Hot-cured Beef

1 kg (2¼ lb) rock salt	
250 g (8¾ oz) juniper berries	
150 g (5¼ oz) sugar	
1 beef tenderloin	
olive oil	

Hot-cured Beef

There are a number of different methods for salt-baking meat. Part cooking, part curing, this recipe results in remarkably tender, delicious beef. This recipe comes from Farzan Contractor, Executive Chef at the Meat & Wine Company, Sydney, Australia.

In a frying pan, lightly toast the juniper berries, then crush them in a mortar. In a large mixing bowl, mix them together with the rock salt and the sugar, then sprinkle with a little olive oil to moisten.

Trim the tenderloin of any fat, then pat with a kitchen towel until it is completely dry. In a baking tray, place enough of the salt mixture that the tenderloin sits entirely upon it, then use the rest of the salt to completely cover the tenderloin, ensuring that no part is visible.

Bake for 20 minutes at 180°C (355°F), then turn the oven down to 40°C (104°F) and let cook for a further 30 minutes. Remove from the oven and immediately break off all of the salt, so that the meat is clearly visible. Wrap the tenderloin tightly in muslin and sit overnight in a cool, dark place.

Once the beef has been cured, it can be served either hot or cold. As with the cured Wagyu, it may be sliced thinly and served with a simple dressing and some herbs, accompanied by crusty bread. Alternatively, you can cut it into thick slices, grill these to bring them up to temperature, and serve with mashed potatoes, green beans and your favourite sauce.

Salt-baked Lamb	
1 lamb loin, boned	
435 g (15⅜ oz) coarse salt	
12 g (¼ oz) fresh parsley, rosemary and oregano, minced	
2 tablespoons cracked black pepper	
375 g (13¼ oz) cups plain (all-purpose) flour	
2 egg whites	
2 tablespoons olive oil	
125 ml (4¼ fl oz) water	

Salt-baked Lamb

Baking meat in a crust of salt not only serves to keep it juicier and prevent it from overcooking, you can also use it to contribute a delicate flavour by adding various herbs and spices to the salt mixture. This recipe is adapted from one featured in *Salt and Pepper* by Michele Anna Jordan.

In a large bowl place the salt, half of the herb mix, the black pepper and the flour. In another bowl, whisk the egg whites with the water until they are frothy. Mix this with the flour until it forms a stiff dough: it will be easier if you have a mixer with a dough hook. Turn it out of the bowl, form into a ball and lightly dust it with flour before wrapping in cling film and leaving to rest for at least 4 hours.

Preheat the oven to 200°C (390F). Heat the olive oil in a heavy saucepan and sear the lamb loin on all sides. Transfer to a plate while you roll out the dough on a floured surface to a thickness of about 5 mm (¼ in). Put the dough on a baking tray and place the lamb in the centre. Sprinkle over the rest of the herbs, then fold the dough around the lamb, pinching the seams to create a perfect seal. Bake for 20 minutes—this should produce perfect, pink lamb. Leave inside the crust for at least 20 minutes and as long as an hour before serving.

The same process can be used to bake a beef tenderloin, or any similar cut of meat. Similarly, the dough can be flavoured with any combination of herbs, spices, lemon zest or other aromatics: each will add their own subtle flavour to the meat.

Chicken in Salt Crust

1 kg (2¼ lb) plain (all-purpose) flour
1 kg (2¼ lb) coarse salt
650 ml (1⅜ pint) water
1 whole organic chicken, approximately 2 kg (4½ lb)
½ lemon
2 cloves garlic

Chicken in Salt Crust

This method is ideal for cooking chicken. Because the entire bird is sealed within the salt crust, no moisture can escape, ensuring that the meat is deliciously juicy and tender. If you have an organic, free-range or corn-fed bird, this is undoubtedly the best way to treat it.

Combine the flour and salt in a large bowl. Make a well in the middle and add most—but not all—of the water. Knead with your hands to make a firm but malleable dough. If the dough is too stiff, add more water.

Once the dough is the correct consistency, cover with cling film and rest for an hour. Roll out the dough on a floured bench to a thickness of about 5 mm (¼ in), then place on a baking tray.

Rinse the chicken and pat dry. Stuff the cavity with half a lemon and two cloves of bruised garlic. Twist the wings of the chicken to sit under the bird and pull the legs away from the body.

Lay the chicken on the dough, breast-side down, and wrap it completely Make sure it is totally covered. Patch any holes that may appear; it is vital that the chicken is completely sealed.

Turn the chicken breast-side up again and cook at 200°C (390°F) for 50 minutes to 1 hour. The crust will bake as hard as clay. Take the chicken out of the oven and rest for at least 30 minutes; the chicken will continue cooking in the crust. Break open the crust at the table, carve and serve.

Like seafood, chicken is a perfect medium for flavoured salt. Try serving lemon salt, tarragon salt or smoked salt at the table to accompany this dish, or perhaps even something a little more adventurous. Using these salts at the table means you can add subtle hints of flavour that complement the basic elements of the dish, without overpowering them.

flavoured brine #2 (recipe on page 58)
1 large or 2 small chickens
salt and pepper
olive oil

Perfect Poultry

Unfortunately, not all chickens are created equal, and economies may demand we use a cheaper bird. Fear not; this recipe will give you such good results that you might swear you were eating the very best organic chicken. This method works equally well on all poultry, including duck. The size of the bird will dictate the brining time; for quail or poussin, half the time should do, for turkey, goose or duck, double.

Rinse the chicken under cold running water. Put a measure of the flavoured brine #2 recipe from page 58 into a large, nonreactive container. Put the chicken in the brine and weight down with a plate to keep submerged. Refrigerate for 6 hours.

Preheat the oven to 245°C (475°F). Remove the chicken from the brine. Discard the brine. Rinse the chicken and pat it dry with paper towels. Season the inside of the chicken lightly with salt and pepper. Truss the chicken. The trussed chicken can be refrigerated for a few hours, but be sure to remove it 30 minutes before cooking.

Oil the chicken—this will keep it from sticking to your roasting pan—and season with salt and pepper. Place the chicken breast-side up into the pan, then into the oven with the legs facing the back of the oven.

Roast for 40 minutes, checking the chicken every 15 minutes. If the chicken is browning unevenly, rotate the pan. Sometimes the brine can remove too much moisture from the skin—if the skin seems to be pulling back from the breast and is cooking too quickly, place a sheet of aluminium foil over the chicken. Do not tent the foil or you will trap in steam. After 40 minutes check the temperature of the chicken with a thermometer between the leg and the thigh. The chicken should be removed from the oven when the temperature reaches 74°C (165°F). Let the chicken rest in a warm spot for 10 minutes before carving. Use the pan juices to make a gravy.

Duck Confit

8 duck legs, about 2 kg (4½ lb)	
1.5 kg (3¼ lb) canned duck or goose fat	
100 g (3½ oz) sea salt	
2 golden shallots, finely chopped	
2 garlic cloves, finely chopped	
2 teaspoons thyme leaves	

Duck Confit

Duck confit, *confit de canard*, is one of the classics of French cuisine. Its roots are centuries old, originating in Gascony but quickly adopted by the rest of France. The technique was born of the necessities of preservation, and has changed little over time. Moisture is drawn from the duck legs with salt, and they are then cooked very slowly in duck fat. They are sealed in the same fat, giving them an overwhelmingly unctuous quality.

Combine the salt, shallot, garlic and thyme in a bowl. Place the duck legs in a single layer in a nonreactive dish, scatter the salt mixture over and rub well all over the duck. Cover with plastic wrap and refrigerate for at least 12 hours.

Brush excess salt mixture from the duck, pat dry with absorbent paper and place in a single layer in a deep roasting pan. Preheat oven to 100°C (230°F). Warm the duck fat in a saucepan over low heat until just melted, then pour over duck legs, ensuring they are completely covered. Bake for 1-1½ hours—the meat should be just coming away from the bone.

Scatter a little salt in the base of an earthenware casserole. Remove the duck from the fat, place in a single layer in the casserole and strain the duck fat. Pour over the duck legs to cover by at least 2 cm (¾ in). Cover and refrigerate until required.

Duck confit is very rich, and a little will go a long way. Serve it in the traditional way, with sliced potatoes that have been crisped in duck fat until golden, or heat the duck legs in a frying pan, shred the meat from the bones and add it to a salad of bitter greens, beetroot (beet), boiled potatoes and green beans.

Roast Pork

Pork is the perfect meat for brining; the process both seasons and tenderises the meat's proteins, making the end result more moist and tastier. The larger the cut and the more dense the flesh, the longer the brining should be. A large shoulder roast may be brined for up to 12 hours, but pork chops would need no more than 4 hours. This is as much to do with the cut as the size; meat that is cut across the grain has far more exposed muscle fibres, making it more porous, and therefore able to absorb the brine more quickly.

Roast Pork

flavoured brine #1 (recipe on page 58)

1 pork shoulder roast, skin removed

Put one portion of the flavoured brine #1 recipe from page 58 in a nonreactive container. Put the pork roast in the brine, cover, and place in the refrigerator for 6–8 hours. Remove the pork from the brine and pat dry with paper towels. Bake at 180°C (355°F) for 20 minutes per 500 g (1⅛ lb) of meat, plus an extra 15 minutes.

Of course, if you are going to roast pork, the thing you want most is crackling. Although salt is essential for good crackling, water is its enemy. Make sure you take the skin from the roast before you brine it, use the following recipe, and the results are virtually guaranteed.

Perfect Crackling

Skin and fat from one pork shoulder roast

Salt

Rinse the skin under cold water and pat it completely dry. Score the skin deeply at 1 cm (⅜ in) intervals. Rub it with salt, cover in cling film and stand for 30 minutes—the salt will extract moisture from the skin. Remove excess salt, dry with paper towels and then sprinkle lightly with more salt. Lay the skin back on the pork roast and bake for the required time.

For an interesting variation, try rubbing the pork skin with smoked salt—the subtle smokiness it imparts will take your crackling from the perfect to the sublime.

Merguez Sausages

2 kg (4½ lb) boneless lamb shoulder, diced into 1-cm (⅜-in) pieces
500 g (1⅛ lb) pork back fat, diced into 1-cm (⅜-in) pieces
3 tablespoons sea salt
2 teaspoons sugar
1 teaspoon chilli flakes
2 tablespoons garlic, minced
200 g (7 oz) roasted red capsicum (peppers), diced
1½ teaspoons cracked black pepper
2 tablespoons Spanish paprika
2 tablespoons fresh oregano, minced
60 ml (2 fl oz) dry red wine, chilled
60 ml (2 fl oz) ice water
prepared sheep casings

Merguez Sausages

These Merguez sausages are of the fresh variety, using salt merely as a flavouring agent, rather than a preservative. This means they need to be eaten soon after making them. They taste so good, however, that you'll find this is not a problem. Use sheep casings—your butcher will have them, or will point you in the right direction.

In a large bowl, combine the lamb, pork fat, salt, sugar, chilli flakes, garlic, roasted capsicum (peppers), black pepper, paprika and oregano and toss to evenly distribute the seasonings. Cover and chill until ready to grind.

Grind the mixture through a meat grinder fitted with the finest plate into a large bowl set over an ice bath. Add the wine and water to the meat mixture and mix in a stand mixer using a paddle attachment, or by hand with a sturdy spoon, until the liquids are incorporated and the mixture has developed a uniform, sticky appearance, about 1 minute on medium speed.

Fry a small portion of the mixture until done to check the flavour and seasoning. If necessary, adjust salt, pepper and other seasonings, then stuff the sausage into the sheep casings with a sausage stuffer and twist into sausages. Refrigerate up to 2 days or freeze up to 2 months until ready to cook.

The making of sausages can soon become addictive. If you are going to pursue it, we recommend purchasing specialised equipment, and reading *Charcuterie: The Craft of Salting, Smoking, and Curing* by Michael Ruhlman, as this will open your eyes to the incredible heights to which the humble sausage can aspire.

Anchovy-spiced Meatballs
200 g (7 zo) beef mince
100 g (3½ oz) pork mince
75 g (2½ oz) bacon, minced
50 g (1¾ oz) anchovy fillets, minced
25 g (⅞ oz) fresh sage
25 g (⅞ oz) fresh oregano
10 g (⅜ oz) fresh parsley
4 medium eggs
1 l (2⅛ pints) anchovy-spiced oil (see page 59)

Anchovy-spiced Meatballs

Technically, there is no salt in this recipe: the saltiness comes from the anchovies, the bacon and the oil in which the meatballs are cooked. Served with a homemade tomato sauce, fresh basil leaves and some parmesan shavings, they make a perfect light meal.

Separate the eggs. Mix the beef, pork, bacon, anchovy and egg yolks in a large mixing bowl. When all the ingredients have been thoroughly incorporated, mix in the herbs so that they are evenly distributed. Roll the mixture into balls of around 75–100 g (2½-3½ oz) and rest overnight in the refrigerator.

Whisk the egg whites until they form soft, white peaks, but remain light in consistency. Warm the anchovy oil to a light simmer, and preheat the oven to 180°C (355°F). Dip the meatballs into the egg white to coat, then fry in the anchovy oil until lightly golden. Place on a baking tray and finish in the oven until cooked through: about 10–15 minutes.

The miracle of anchovies is that they do not necessarily make things taste "fishy". Cooked with other ingredients they transform into a salty, savoury flavour that complements all sorts of different foods, from beef and lamb to beans and pasta dishes. Even people who profess to loathe anchovies will not know they're there—they will only know that *something* tastes delicious.

Vegetables

When preparing vegetables, less is usually more. Think of a tomato picked from the vine and still warm, some extra-virgin olive oil and a sprinkling of fleur de sel. Potatoes that have been cut into sticks, fried until golden, then lightly salted. Salad leaves with a simple vinaigrette of salt, oil and vinegar.

This is the way vegetables are best served. The less they are cooked, the more of their essential goodness they retain. And salt is there to bring out the flavour, not to change it or mask it. As the great French chef, Fernand Point, said, "If the creator has taken the trouble to give us these exquisite things, we should prepare them with care and present them with ceremony."

Perfect French Fries

3 large, waxy potatoes
vegetable oil
sea salt

Perfect French Fries

If you have cooked a perfect steak, then there are only two things you could do to make it better. Accompany it with some tarragon salt (page 47) and serve it with the perfect French fries.

Peel the potatoes. Square them up by trimming them on four sides and two ends, then cut into uniform slices a little less than 1-cm (⅜-in) thick. Cut these slices at intervals of a little less than 1 cm (⅜ in), making them into uniform sticks. Wash under cold running water and dry well in a cloth.

Heat the oil to 170°C (338°) and deep-fry the potatoes for 7–8 minutes, until they just begin to colour. Drain them on kitchen paper. Just before serving reheat the oil to 180°C (355°F) and fry the chips until they are golden. Drain on kitchen paper and transfer to a bowl. Sprinkle generously with sea salt, tossing with a spoon to ensure all the fries are properly seasoned.

An unsalted French fry is virtually inconceivable. The fries need to be seasoned a few seconds after they have come from the fryer, so that there is still a small amount of oil on their surface for the salt to cling to. The salt you use should be a reasonably fine sea salt that will stick to the fries evenly but not in excessive amounts. And the fries must be served immediately, before they have a chance to cool or go soft.

Potatoes and Garlic

1½ kg (3¼ lb) small new potatoes
1 garlic bulb
2 bay leaves
sea salt
1 teaspoon black peppercorns

Potatoes and Garlic

Traditionally, the potatoes and garlic are cooked in an unglazed clay pot that needs to be thoroughly seasoned by soaking overnight in cold water before use, and then heated very gradually. But the end result is more than worth it. This recipe is inspired by one found in Jody Vassallo's *Salt and Pepper*.

Scrub the potatoes but do not peel. Layer the bottom of an unglazed clay pot with salt. Add the potatoes—they should cover the bottom in a single layer. Lay on the bay leaves. Peel the garlic cloves and layer them on top of the potatoes, then sprinkle with more salt and the peppercorns. Put the lid on the pot.

Put the pot in a cold oven and slowly bring the heat up to 200°C (390°F). Bake for 1½ hours. Test the potatoes with a skewer; it should go all the way through with no resistance. Take the pot from the oven and place it on a trivet, leaving the lid on until you are ready to serve.

Tomatoes

Tomatoes. Olive oil. Sea salt. You could easily leave it at that. However, the addition of a few garlic cloves and some herbs will raise your tomatoes from the fantastic to the sublime.

Slow-roasted Cherry Tomatoes

cherry tomatoes
garlic
olive oil
sea salt
fennel, oregano, basil, thyme

Pour a little olive oil in the bottom of a baking dish. Cut the cherry tomatoes in half and layer cut-side up so that they fill the baking dish. Scatter with unpeeled garlic cloves. Drizzle liberally with olive oil and sprinkle with a generous amount of sea salt. Chop a handful of the mixed herbs and toss over the tomatoes.

Heat the oven to 110°C (230°F). Bake the tomatoes for 3–4 hours—they should be shrivelled but still retain a certain amount of moisture. Serve warm, or transfer the entire contents of the dish, including all the juices, to a covered container and store in the refrigerator.

Baking in salt is not confined to meat and fish. Vegetables, too, benefit from the process. During the cooking process the salt draws out some of the water, thereby concentrating the flavours.

Salt-roasted Vine Tomatoes

1 kg (2¼ lb) coarse rock salt
1 dozen fresh vine-ripened tomatoes
15 ml (½ fl oz) extra-virgin olive oil
20 g (¾ oz) sage
20 g (¾ oz) basil
20 g (¾ oz) oregano

Take an ovenproof baking tray and layer it with 25 mm (1 in) of the coarse rock salt. Place the vine ripened tomatoes with the green vines attached to the individual tomato over the salt, setting them nicely on the base of salt. Make sure none of the tomatoes touch each other; they should all be separated, with salt in between them.

Sprinkle with a slight dash of olive oil, pour the rest of the salt over the tomatoes until they are completely covered. Place into the oven at 150°C (300°F) for about 1 hour, then turn the temperature down to 100°C (210°F) and leave in the oven for another 2 hours. Take them out of oven, gently separate the salt on the top of the tomatoes, and once removed from the salt, let them cool on a wire cooling rack.

Separately chop up all the herbs and mix with a splash of extra-virgin olive oil, then sprinkle over the tomatoes. Serve with fresh buffalo mozzarella and a handful of wild rocket, drizzle over some extra-virgin olive oil and garnish with slivers of white anchovy.

Like so many of the other recipes, this method works equally well on a range of different vegetables. Try it with zucchinis (courgettes) or Spanish onions, and take it from there.

Caponata

A Sicilian dish, caponata illustrates two important things. First, the value of salt in drawing out moisture and removing bitterness and second, the way that saltiness can come from other ingredients, in this case both capers and olives. It is also delicious, served either hot or cold, as a side dish, or with fresh, crusty bread as a meal in itself.

Caponata

135 g (4¾ oz) peeled eggplant (aubergine), cubed

1 teaspoon sea salt

4 tablespoons olive oil

100 g (3½ oz) onion, chopped

65 g (2¼ oz) green capsicum (pepper), chopped

65 g (2¼ oz) red capsicum (pepper), chopped

50 g (1¾ oz) celery, chopped

500 g (1⅛ lb) drained canned tomatoes, chopped, juice reserved

½ teaspoon cracked black pepper

½ teaspoon dried oregano

½ teaspoon dried basil

2 garlic cloves, minced

1 tablespoon fresh Italian parsley, chopped

75 g (2½ oz) pitted kalamata olives, chopped

2 tablespoons capers, drained

Place the eggplant (aubergine) in a colander, sprinkle with salt and let drain for 1 hour. Heat 2 tablespoons of oil in large flameproof casserole. Pat the eggplant (aubergine) dry and add to the casserole dish. Sauté over medium heat until soft and lightly browned. Remove the eggplant and set aside. Add the remaining oil, then onion, peppers and celery. Sauté over medium heat until the vegetables are softened. Return the eggplant (aubergine) to the casserole and add the tomatoes, capsicum (pepper), oregano, basil, garlic, parsley, olives and capers. Simmer for around 30 minutes, so that the vegetables are tender. If the mixture starts sticking while cooking, add some of the reserved tomato juice in small amounts. Transfer to a serving dish, and serve either warm or cold.

Chilli-salted Snake Beans

These beans illustrate just how much most vegetables will benefit from a little seasoning, a little spice and a touch of salt. The recipe is adapted from one found in Donna Hay's *Off The Shelf*.

Chilli-salted Snake Beans

500 g (1⅛ lb) snake beans

2 teaspoons sesame oil

3 large red chillies

2 garlic cloves

½ teaspoon cracked black pepper

½ teaspoon sea salt

Steam the beans over boiling water until they are tender. Slice the chillies and garlic, and in a hot wok, fry with the remaining ingredients, then toss through the cooked beans.

Simple Salad

The word "salad" originates from the Romans, who had a habit of salting their greens. Now we are more likely to mix up a vinaigrette to season salad leaves with. This version is even simpler: just add the seasonings one at a time, and toss. As an accompaniment to the perfect steak (see page 94) and fries (page 106), it would be, well, perfect.

Simple Salad

115 g (4 oz) assorted lettuce

35 g (1¼ oz) bitter greens such as rocket, pepper-cress, nasturtium leaves

extra-virgin olive oil

lemon juice or red wine vinegar

fleur de sel

cracked black pepper

Rinse the lettuce and the bitter greens and dry in a cloth. Place in a large bowl. Sprinkle generously with fleur de sel and toss gently. Add a good splash of olive oil and toss with a small amount of lemon juice or red wine vinegar.

Green Papaya Salad

Arguably one of the most popular dishes in Thailand, green papaya salad is traditionally made in a large earthenware mortar, using a wooden pestle and a spatula. If your mortar and pestle is not large enough to fit the whole salad, you can use it to pound the first few ingredients, then transfer them to a large bowl before adding the rest.

Green Papaya Salad

285 g (10 oz) shredded green papaya

6 snake beans

1 lime

1½ tablespoons palm sugar

1 garlic clove

1½ tablespoons fish sauce

1 tablespoon dried shrimp

2 red chillies

5 cherry tomatoes, halved

2 tablespoons roasted peanuts

In the mortar, crush the garlic clove, then add the beans and tomatoes. Pound these a few times with the pestle—just enough to bruise the beans and release some juice from the tomatoes. Add the chillies and crush to release the oil. Add the green papaya, dried shrimp, peanuts, fish sauce, lime juice and palm sugar. Using the pestle to mix and a spatula to push, ensure that all the ingredients are fully combined. Serve with sticky rice.

Greens in Oyster Sauce

The classic Chinese combination of greens and salty oyster sauce.

Greens in Oyster Sauce

bok choi, Chinese broccoli, broccoli or green beans

2 teaspoons sesame oil

2 tablespoons shredded ginger

80 ml (2¾ fl oz) oyster sauce

2 tablespoons brown sugar

80 ml (2¾ fl oz) Chinese rice wine

Steam the greens until tender. Place all of the other ingredients in a hot wok and simmer until thick. Place the greens on a serving plate and pour over the sauce.

opposite Ingredients like anchovies and capers provide the salty element in a classic green sauce (see the recipe on page 119).

Sauces

In Asian cooking salt is rarely applied directly to food and it is rarely used at the table. Saltiness comes most frequently from condiments—soy sauce, fish sauce, miso—that have salt as an essential component.

So it is with cooking: we can add "invisible" salt, as it were, by incorporating a whole range of different foods—such as olives, capers, anchovies or bacon—into dishes as they are being cooked. The effect is often subtle, but delicious. The classic chicken liver paté, for example, gains a depth of flavour from the addition of capers, though one would never know to look at it. Many soups benefit greatly from a small handful of diced bacon sautéed along with the other ingredients. And although there are many people who would never knowingly eat an anchovy, they are often included in savoury dishes such as stews or braises to give the sauce a little something extra.

The other place that salty ingredients shine is in sauces. Every type of cuisine has its salty sauces—from Thai dipping sauce to salsa verde—they are an ideal way to add a little zing to any type of food. Some use fewer ingredients than others, and indeed any of them can be made to suit your tastes: just add a little more of one thing, a little less of another. The key is to experiment, to taste and to enjoy—the following recipes will provide a base for you to expand your repertoire.

Nuoc Cham

4 red chillies
2 garlic cloves
2 limes
1 teaspoon palm sugar
1 tablespoon hot water
1 tablespoon vinegar
5 tablespoons fish sauce

Nuoc Cham

Fish sauce is central to Thai cuisine. Here it is used in *nuoc cham*, the classic Thai dipping sauce. There are very few things that nuoc cham won't improve: start with salt-baked prawns or homemade spring rolls and take it from there.

Pound the garlic in a mortar. Slice the chillies and add them to the mortar a little at a time, processing until you have a fine paste. Peel the limes and cut them into sections, then add them to the mortar along with the palm sugar. Remove to a small bowl and add the water, vinegar and fish sauce. Mix well and stand for half an hour for the flavours to combine.

Another, even simpler idea, is to mix a quantity of fish sauce with an equal amount of sugar, creating a thick, sweet, salty slurry. It is excellent when accompanying green mangoes, and it adds the perfect complement to anything which is slightly bitter or sour.

Black Bean Sauce

1½ tablespoons fermented black beans
2 teaspoons garlic, finely chopped
2 teaspoons ginger, finely chopped
1½ teaspoons red chilli, finely chopped
1 tablespoon sesame oil
2 teaspoons rice vinegar
1½ teaspoons sugar
1 star anise
150 ml (5 fl oz) chicken stock
1 tablespoon dark soy sauce
1 sprig of coriander (cilantro), roughly chopped
3 spring onions (scallions), finely sliced
1 teaspoon cornflour

Black Bean Sauce

Black bean sauce uses no added salt because the fermented black beans, which make up the base of its flavour, are very salty indeed. They can be bought from any Asian supermarket.

Quickly rinse the black beans to remove some of the saltiness. In the sesame oil, fry the garlic, ginger and chillies until fragrant. Add the black beans, sugar, vinegar and star anise and simmer for another 2 minutes. Then add the stock, cooking over a low heat for about 5 minutes. Add the coriander (cilantro) and the spring onions (scallions). Finally, mix the cornflour with a little cold water to make a thin paste, then whisk this into the sauce. Cook for another minute, so that the sauce reaches the right consistency, then transfer to a sealed container. Store in the refrigerator for up to 1 week.

Black bean sauce will make almost anything taste like a Chinese meal—this is a good thing—but it goes particularly well with pork spare ribs.

Soy Sauce

2.5 kg (5½ lb) soya beans
1 kg (2¼ lb) plain (all-purpose) flour
5 l (10½ pints) of water
1.5 kg (3¼ lb) salt

Soy Sauce

The idea of making one's own soy sauce might seem extravagant. But as an illustration of the transformative powers of salt it is at once educational and satisfying. What's more, the results will be unlike any of the commercial products you can buy in the supermarket. Chances are, they will be better.

Boil the soya beans until they are reduced to a purée. Add the flour and knead until you have a thick dough. Leave it in a cool dark place for 2 days, then hang the container in a draught for a week. A yellow mould will appear on the dough. Stir the salt into the water and put into a clear jar. Leave it in the sun, and when it is warm to the touch, put the dough in the jar. Leave the jar uncovered for a day, then pound the mixture vigorously with a stick.

Repeat every day for 1 month; as the mixture ages it will turn black. Leave the jar in a sunny place, uncovered, for 4–5 months without stirring, but cover if the weather is bad. Pour the sauce into sterilised bottles and seal.

2 tablespoons white miso
3 tablespoons olive oil
1 tablespoon lemon juice
2 tablespoons tahini
water

All-purpose Miso Dressing

It is hard to believe just how versatile the humble soya bean is: it can be made into sauce, milk, curd or paste, it is incredibly nutritious, and in its fermented form provides a flavour base that is essential to both Chinese and Japanese cooking.

Miso, in which the beans are fermented with cooked rice or barley and left to mature for up to two years, comes in a range of different colours and sweetnesses, depending on the combination of grains: generally, the lighter the colour, the more delicate the flavour.

This recipe uses "white" miso to create a multi-purpose liquid that can be used as a dressing, soup or glaze, depending on the consistency you make it.

Whisk together the first four ingredients. Add the water as required to achieve the desired consistency. Use as a dressing for salads or vegetables.

Once you have the basic blend, this recipe can be altered in a number of different ways, for a range of different uses. Replace the lemon juice with soy sauce, for example, and the olive oil with stock, and you have the base for a soup, or a perfect poaching broth for vegetables. If you replace the lemon juice with sugar and omit the olive oil, then stir over heat to thicken, you have an ideal glaze for salmon, or a sauce to pour over just about anything.

Umeboshi and Parsley Dressing

2 umeboshi plums, pits removed
1 teaspoon parsley, minced
1/4 teaspoon onion, grated
1/4 teaspoon sesame oil, heated (optional)
190 ml (6½ fl oz) water

Umeboshi and Parsley Dressing

The Japanese love umeboshi, the salted and pickled plum—but being both very sour and very salty, it is an acquired taste for Westerners. But the health benefits imputed to umeboshi and their unique taste make them worth seeking out. This salty dressing is a good way to explore the extreme taste of the umeboshi, because you can use just a little at first.

Place the umeboshi plums in a suribachi and grind to a smooth paste. Add the parsley and onion, grind again. Add the oil and mix to a purée. Add the water and purée again.

A suribachi is a Japanese style pestle and mortar. Its ridged inside surface makes it ideal for grinding roasted sesame seeds and making dressings such as this one. Otherwise, use a small food processor.

Green Sauce

curly and flat-leaf parsley
anchovies
garlic
capers
extra-virgin olive oil
cracked black pepper

Green Sauce

Like tapenade, green sauce has so many variations that a definitive recipe is impossible. But the essential constituents are those listed above. If you have half a bunch each of curly and flat-leaf parsley, you can adjust the quantities of the other ingredients to suit your taste. After that, the addition of other herbs, mustard, even cubes of bread soaked in vinegar, is perfectly acceptable.

Coarsely chop the parsley by hand, then finely chop the anchovies and garlic and roughly chop the capers (if they are very small, leave them whole) then put everything in a small bowl. Pour olive oil over the mixture until it reaches a loose slurry. Grind over a little fresh black pepper.

If you have any mint, dill and/or tarragon, your green sauce will benefit from their addition, but they are not essential.

Tapenade

Tapenade is the classic Mediterranean dish, redolent of sun, sea and earth. This version is pared back to its essentials, the classic salty triumvirate of olives, anchovies and capers, enlivened with a touch of garlic and herbs.

Tapenade

200 g (7 oz) black olives, stoned

10 anchovy fillets

50 g (1¾ oz) capers

2 cloves of garlic

25 g (⅞ oz) fresh basil

sprigs of fresh thyme

Rinse both the anchovies and the capers if they have been preserved in salt, and place all the ingredients in a food processor. Blend briefly: the tapenade should have a grainy texture, being neither too chunky, nor blended to a purée.

Anchovy Paste

Truly, there is no middle ground with anchovies. You either love them or you hate them. And if you love them, you'll find this sauce irresistible.

Anchovy Paste

7 garlic cloves

1 tin anchovies in oil

250 ml (8½ fl oz) extra-virgin olive oil

red wine vinegar

cracked black pepper

Using a pestle and mortar, crush the garlic with a little black pepper, then add the drained anchovies. Stir in the oil a little at a time; when most of it has been added, splash in a little red wine vinegar. Test for taste and consistency, adding more oil and vinegar if necessary. The paste may be stiff enough for spreading, or loose enough to use as a dressing, depending on your preference.

Caper Mayonnaise

Sometimes you want a sauce that has the salty tang of capers, but without the strong taste of anchovies, garlic or parsley. Enter caper mayonnaise, which is a particularly versatile condiment, based on a classic French mayonnaise.

Caper Mayonnaise

2 egg yolks
sea salt
white pepper
300 ml (10 fl oz) olive oil
2 tablespoons pickled capers
1 tablespoon tarragon, chopped

Make sure all the ingredients are at room temperature. Put the egg yolks, a pinch each of salt and white pepper, and a splash of brine from the pickled capers into a medium bowl. Stir quickly with a whisk or a wooden spoon. As soon as the mixture is smooth, blend in a tablespoon of the olive oil, drop by drop, along with a few more drops of brine. Add another tablespoon of oil, drop by drop, taking care to beat the sauce against the side of the bowl. Now the oil can be added in a thin stream as you continue beating. When all of the oil has been added, roughly chop the capers and add them to the mayonnaise. Check for taste and consistency, adding a little more brine or lemon juice. Finally, stir through the chopped tarragon.

Salt Pork Gravy

The salt pork from page 64 has many uses—add it in place of bacon or pancetta to soups and stews, or make a classic dish of beans and salt pork. Perhaps the best use of it, however, is this rich, thick, salty gravy.

Salt Pork Gravy

500 g (1⅛ lb) lean salt pork, cut into 1.5-cm (½-in) thick strips
3 tablespoons plain (all-purpose) flour
salt
pepper
500 ml (17 fl oz) milk

Freshen the pork by covering with cold water in a large frying pan and bringing to boil. Drain and rinse with cold water. Fry the salt pork on medium high until crisp on both sides. Remove and drain most of the fat from the pan, leaving about 3 tablespoons. Add 3 tablespoons flour to make a roux. Cook to a light caramel colour, then slowly stir in the milk to make a cream gravy. Add salt and pepper and the crisp fried salt pork.

opposite Salt enhances the flavour of chocolate in this dark chocolate mousse with olive oil and sea salt (see recipe on page 125), as well as providing the perfect contrast to the sweetness of salted caramel macarons (page 132).

Sweet

In Thailand, if you buy a piece of fruit at a roadside fruit stand, you will receive a small packet of *prik-kab-klua*, salt that has been mixed with sugar and chillies. Try and you will see why.

Because it makes the fruit taste better.

It is a strange but simple rule that a little salt makes almost everything taste better. The reasons are complex, and are explained in more detail in the chapter entitled "That Salty Taste", beginning on page 166. But here, all we need do is try the following recipes. Some of them may sound strange, outlandish even, but don't be put off. After all, salty sweets are nothing new: the French are believed to have created salted caramel over 400 years ago, and the Chinese made salted egg custards more than 4,000 years before that.

And now salted desserts are virtually standard fare. Variations of salted caramels and salty chocolate appear on restaurant menus around the world as chefs have come to realise that salt and sweet together are not merely a gimmick, but rather a way of complementing flavours and bringing about exciting combinations that are both innovative and tasty.

As always, these recipes are just the beginning—use your imagination, experiment, and a whole new world of tastes may open up to you, too.

1 day-old baguette
70% cocoa solids chocolate, chopped
extra-virgin olive oil
fleur de sel

Pan con Chocolate y Sal

The combination of bread, chocolate and salt might initially sound outlandish, but it has long been a hugely popular treat in Spain: think of it as a grown-up version of Nutella on toast. Use your own homemade bread in place of the baguette, if you want, and experiment with different types of chocolate, salt and olive oil. Just remember to use the best quality you can find.

Preheat the oven to 200°C (390°F). Slice the baguette into thick diagonal slices and lay on a baking tray. Drizzle very lightly with olive oil. Heat the bread until it just begins to brown. Remove from the oven and top each slice with chocolate. Return to the oven until the chocolate has barely melted; a minute or two will be enough.

Remove from the oven and transfer to a serving plate. Drizzle with a little more of the olive oil and sprinkle with fleur de sel.

Here is also an ideal place to use some of your homemade salt: both vanilla salt and coconut salt will add their own particular twist to the flavour.

| 250 ml (8½ fl oz) heavy cream |
| 225 g (8 oz) 70% cocoa solids chocolate |
| extra-virgin olive oil |
| Maldon salt |

Chocolate Mousse with Olive Oil and Salt

This dessert is the perfect illustration of just how well chocolate and salt go together. Strong, dark chocolate can be almost bitter, and the salt serves to counteract the bitterness, bringing out the pure chocolate flavour, and adding a delicate crunch to the silky smooth mousse. This recipe is adapted from *The New Spanish Table* by Anya von Bremzen.

Put the cream in a small, heavy saucepan and heat until almost boiling. Chop the chocolate finely, either in a food processor or with a knife. Place in a metal bowl and pour the hot cream over all at once. Let the cream stand for 2–3 minutes while the chocolate melts. Using a rubber spatula, gently stir the cream slowly in a circular motion from the centre to the side of the bowl until all the chocolate is incorporated. Transfer the mixture to a clean bowl, cover with cling film and let sit at room temperature for at least 4 hours.

To serve, use a melon baller to scoop the mousse into chilled martini glasses or decorative shallow bowls. Pour 2–3 teaspoons of the olive oil around the mousse, and drizzle a tiny amount over the top. Sprinkle generously with Maldon salt.

Maldon salt is specified here because its texture is ideal, but you might also try Murray River pink salt or Hawaiian 'Alaea salt—their colour will add to the visual appeal of the dish. And, if you were feeling adventurous, you could even serve it with a sprinkling of smoked chilli salt.

Caramel

Salted caramel has a long history. The famous American saltwater taffy was indeed made with saltwater direct from the sea. In Brittany, heavily salted butter caramels have been made for over 400 years. Here, you will find two variations on salt caramel: a brittle caramel that can be broken up and used in the ice cream on page 139—as well as for a topping or garnish—and a soft salted-butter caramel.

Salted Caramel

100 g (3½ oz) sugar

¾ teaspoon fleur de sel

Cover a baking tray with a silicone mat, or lightly grease it with oil. Place the sugar in a medium-sized, heavy-based saucepan and heat without stirring over a moderate heat. When the edges of the sugar begin to melt, gently stir the liquefied sugar into the centre of the pan, until all the sugar has dissolved. Continue to cook, stirring occasionally, until the sugar is a caramel colour and smells as though it is just about to burn.

Working quickly, sprinkle the fleur de sel over the caramel without stirring and then pour the caramel on to the baking tray, tilting and rotating the sheet so that the caramel forms a thin even layer. Set aside to cool and harden.

Vanilla-salted Soft Caramel

250 g (8¾ oz) caster sugar

100 ml (3½ fl oz) milk

80 g (2¾ oz) honey

1 vanilla bean, split in half

150 g (5¼ oz) unsalted butter

vanilla salt

Put all of the ingredients, except the butter, into a heavy saucepan and bring to the boil, stirring constantly with a wooden spoon. Add the butter piece by piece until it is all incorporated.

Reduce the heat to low and cook until it reaches 120°C (248°F). Lightly oil a mould of the shape you desire—it should be at least 18 cm (7 in) in diameter. Remove the vanilla bean, then pour the caramel into the mould. Allow to cool, but before it is completely set, sprinkle the vanilla salt on top. Cut the caramel to the desired size pieces, and store in a sealed container in the refrigerator.

This recipe was provided by Stephane Jégat, Executive Chef at Kobe Jones, Sydney, Australia.

Caramel and Dark Chocolate Truffles
625 g (1⅜ lb) bitter chocolate
80 g (2¾ oz) sugar
2 tablespoons of water
165 ml (5½ fl oz) cream
¼ teaspoon fleur de sel
45 g (1½ oz) cocoa powder
additional fleur de sel

Caramel and Dark Chocolate Truffles

American President Barack Obama is reported to have developed a taste for salted caramels covered in chocolate. You could make your own, using the soft caramel recipe on the previous page, or you could try these truffles. Either way, you can't go wrong.

Melt one-third of the chocolate in a metal bowl over simmering water. Stir until smooth.

Combine the sugar and the water in a saucepan and stir over a medium heat until the sugar dissolves. Increase the heat and boil until the syrup becomes a deep caramel colour—it will take about 5 minutes. Remove from the heat and add the cream, then stir over a very low heat until the caramel is smooth. Mix the caramel and ¼ teaspoon of fleur de sel into the melted chocolate. Chill for at least 3 hours, so that the truffle mixture is firm.

Place the cocoa in a bowl. Using 1 tablespoon of filling for each truffle, roll into balls and then coat with cocoa. Arrange on a baking tray, cover and chill overnight.

Melt the rest of the chocolate over simmering water and stir until smooth. Working quickly, dip each truffle into the chocolate using a fork. Allow excess chocolate to drip off, then place the truffles on a baking tray covered with foil. When all the truffles are coated, sprinkle lightly with additional fleur de sel. Stand for at least an hour to let the coating set.

Bananas Flambé

2 bananas
2 tablespoons packed brown sugar
unsalted butter
Grand Marnier, rum or Cointreau
1 Himalayan salt block

Bananas Flambé

The combination of the heated salt block and the *flambé* might make this recipe seem almost like a novelty. Rest assured, you'll only need to taste the result to realise that it's no gimmick; the buttery, sugary, salty sauce adds a sophistication that bananas rarely achieve on their own.

Heat the salt block gradually on the stove top, starting on low and raising the heat every 10 minutes (for tips on heating the Himalayan salt block safely, see page 19).

When the salt block is very hot, slice the bananas and have all your other ingredients ready. Place a knob of unsalted butter in the middle of the salt block and then add the bananas, tossing the butter over the bananas with a spatula. Sprinkle the brown sugar over the top.

Turn off the heat and splash with the alcohol, then carefully ignite with a long kitchen match.

Divide the bananas between two serving plates and serve immediately, accompanied by vanilla ice cream with Murray River pink salt (see recipe on page 138).

The flambé is something that has fallen out of fashion, perhaps unfairly. Flaming fruit with alcohol is a great way to caramelise the natural sugars in the fruit, and to impart different flavours. It looks cool too.

Fruit Roasted in Salt

It is not surprising that fruit can be baked in salt: after all, virtually everything else can be! The lavender in this recipe not only protects the delicate fruit during the cooking process, it also imparts a subtle perfume. Baking times will vary depending on the type of fruit—a firm pear will take longer to cook than a ripe peach—so it is best to bake only one type at a time.

Wash the fruit and dry it thoroughly. Put a layer of salt in the bottom of a baking tray. Wrap 3 or 4 of the lavender branches around each piece of fruit and place on the salt, leaving plenty of space between. Fill the tray carefully with more salt until all of the fruit is covered. Bake at 200°C (390°F) for about 20 minutes.

Remove from the oven and let cool for 10 minutes. Carefully break open the salt crust and extract the fruit. Brush off any remaining salt, peel and slice the fruit before serving.

Of course, you don't always have to go to the trouble of baking fruit to improve its flavour. A sprinkling of prik-kab-klua, the Thai combination of salt, sugar and chilli from page 49, can spice up sliced raw fruit such as melon, pear, mango or apple. Both watermelon and fresh, ripe strawberries can be topped with a little sea salt and a touch of ground black pepper. Or try Indian black salt (kala namak) on the melon, or truffle salt on the strawberries.

250 g (8¾ oz) plain (all-purpose) flour
125 g (4½ oz) butter, chilled, chopped
80 g (2¾ oz) caster sugar
1 egg yolk
1 pinch of salt
1 tablespoon chilled water

Sweet Short-crust Pastry

Salt does the same thing in pastry as it does in all of cooking—it enhances flavour, it rounds out the different flavours and it ensures that everything comes together.

Combine the flour, butter and sugar in a food processor. Process until the mixture resembles fine breadcrumbs. Add the egg yolk and chilled water. Process until the dough just comes together.

Turn the pastry onto a lightly floured surface and knead until just smooth. Shape into a disc. Wrap in baking paper and refrigerate for 30 minutes. Blind bake at 180°C (355°F) for 12 minutes.

It may not seem like much, but the pinch of salt in short-crust pastry will make a dramatic improvement in its taste. The pastry can be used with all kinds of fillings. Try layering it with some of the pastry cream from page 136, sliced salt-baked fruit and a glaze of apricot jam thinned with hot water.

Meringues

80 g (2¾ oz) light brown sugar	
4 egg whites	
100 g (3½ oz) caster sugar	
fine sea salt	

Meringues

Because they are made with brown sugar as well as caster sugar, these meringues are a darker colour than usual, and the pinch of salt will make a noticeable difference to the flavour.

Heat the oven to 120°C (248°F). Line two baking trays with baking paper. Sift the brown sugar into a bowl with a good pinch of sea salt. Beat the egg whites until soft peaks form, then add the caster sugar in three equal portions, beating until the whites are glossy and stiff. Continue beating and gently sift the brown sugar on to the egg whites, ceasing as soon as it is incorporated.

Use a tablespoon to place dollops of meringue on the baking tray, leaving plenty of space between.

Bake for 50 minutes, then turn off the oven and, leaving the door slightly ajar, let the meringues cool before removing.

You can fill these meringues with the pastry cream from page 136, serve them with the salted caramel ice cream, or join them together with whipped cream to accompany the roasted fruit from page 129.

Salted Caramel Macarons

The *caramel a la fleur de sel macaron* was invented by the Parisan *pâtissier* Pierre Hermé in the 1980s, and has since become famous among macaron lovers. Don't be intimidated by the macaron's reputation as being difficult to make: the process is quite simple—the secret lies in the meringue, which should be firm but not *too* firm.

For the Macarons

500 g (1⅛ lb) ground almonds	
900 g (2 lb) icing sugar	
440 g (15½ oz) egg white	
120 g (4¼ oz) sugar	
fleur de sel	

For the Caramel

200 g (7 oz) sugar	
1 vanilla pod, split	
200 g (7 oz) cream	
140 g (5 oz) unsalted butter, chilled	
¾ teaspoon fleur de sel	

Sieve the ground almonds and icing sugar into a mixing bowl. Using an electric mixer, whisk the egg whites at high speed until you see a line made by the whisk going round. Add the sugar while the mixer is at medium speed and beat until the meringue is stiff. Fold the meringue into the dry ingredients: do not overfold it.

Pipe the mixture onto a silicone mat or an oiled baking tray—they should be around 3 cm (1 in) in diameter. If the mixture is too thick, you will see a tip sticking up from the balls: give the tray a small tap to ensure a nice smooth surface.

Leave the piped macarons out for 30 minutes so that a skin can form. Bake them at 160°C (320°F) in a fan oven for approximately 14-16 minutes. Remove them from the oven and sprinkle each macaron with a little fleur de sel and leave to cool on a wire rack.

Let the macarons cool until you have made the caramel for the filling.

Cook the sugar in a large, heavy pot, stirring all the time, until it is an even caramel. Scrape the seeds from the vanilla pod and add both to the caramel. Warm the cream, then add a little at a time: be careful as it may splatter. Add the fleur de sel. Stir thoroughly, then cool the mixture to just over blood heat. Cut the chilled butter into cubes and stir in one at a time using an immersion blender. Blend until the caramel is smooth and glossy. Cover the surface of the caramel with cling film to prevent a skin from forming and chill in the refrigerator until needed.

When the macarons and the caramel have cooled completely, sandwich two macarons together with a little caramel and leave to set.

This basic macaron recipe can be adapted to any flavour you like: some will benefit from the addition of salt and some will not.

From the Dairy

Cheese has been called one of the great achievements of civilisation. It is certainly true that from two humble ingredients, milk and salt, an astonishing variety of outcomes can occur, from a silky mozzarella to a creamy brie, a nutty, yellow havarti to a salty, pungent Roquefort.

And though the resulting cheeses may make it seem that cheese-making is a complex and difficult art, known only to a few, the fact is that cheese can be made by anybody. True, one will probably never be able to reproduce the classic cheeses, which rely on very specific processes, locations and the conditions under which they are aged. But anybody can make cheese at home, and indeed everybody should.

Not just cheese, either. Making your own ice cream, or your own butter, is both satisfying and easy. Importantly, it also reminds us that food does not have to come from the supermarket, and that basic processes devised and used over the centuries still have a vital part to play in modern life. And it reminds us that salt, as always, is an essential part of almost all the food we eat.

Pastry Cream

250 ml (8½ fl oz) milk	
60 g (2 oz) sugar	
a pinch of salt	
2 large egg yolks	
2½ tablespoons cornflour	
½ vanilla pod	

Pastry Cream

Sometimes, just a pinch of salt in the right place can make a world of difference.

Scrape the seeds from the vanilla pod. Put the seeds and the pod into a large, heavy saucepan along with the rest of the ingredients. Stir constantly with a whisk as you bring the mixture to the boil. Boil for 1 minute, at which point the mixture will have thickened and the whisk will leave tracks as you stir.

Take the pan off the heat. With a rubber spatula, push the cream through a sieve into a bowl. Allow to cool, then cover with cling film, pressing it down on to the surface of the cream. Use within 3 days.

This recipe shows how salt can be "invisible" yet integral: no one will know it's there, yet they will taste the difference. The trick is to use just enough to bring out the flavours and no more.

Dulce de Leche

2 l (4¼ pints) whole milk
550 g (19½ oz) cups sugar
1 vanilla pod
¾ teaspoon sea salt

Dulce de Leche

Before you reach the cheese course, you need to ensure your sweet tooth has been satisfied. And if this doesn't do it, nothing will. Very popular throughout South America and Mexico, *dulce de leche* is—as the name suggests—little more than sweet milk. The addition of a little salt tempers the sweetness and brings out the caramel flavour; another example of how salt has the power to enhance almost any food.

Put all the ingredients in a heavy saucepan and stir over a medium heat. After about 30 minutes the mixture will begin to thicken, and you can remove the vanilla pod (which may be rinsed and used again). Reduce the heat to low and continue cooking, stirring frequently, until the mixture turns caramel in colour and becomes very thick; it will take about 2½ hours. Remove from the heat and keep stirring until the mixture cools. Transfer to a container, cover and chill.

❧

Dulce de leche is especially good when made with fresh goat's milk, if you can get it. Indeed, all of the following recipes are best made with fresh whole milk or cream; if it is not too far, this is worth travelling to country areas to obtain.

Vanilla Ice Cream with Murray River Pink Salt

250 ml (8½ fl oz) cream
250 ml (8½ fl oz) milk
85 g (3 oz) sugar
1½ vanilla pods
5 egg yolks
½ teaspoon Murray River pink salt

Vanilla Ice Cream with Murray River Pink Salt

Salty ice cream? Yes, it does work! Particularly in combination with overly sweet desserts—the salt helps cut through the sweetness and brings out the flavours. But you do need to be careful, as there is a fine line between salty and *too* salty: add the salt a little at a time, tasting as you go.

In a saucepan, heat the cream, milk, sugar and the split vanilla pods. Whisk together the egg yolks in a separate bowl. When the cream mixture is scorched but not boiling, pour half of the liquid over the eggs, stir to combine, then pour the mixture back into the saucepan.

Cook over a medium heat, stirring regularly with a wooden spoon until the mixture coats the back of the spoon. Pass the mixture through a fine sieve into a bowl set over ice and stir until cool. Transfer to an ice-cream maker and churn until firm peaks form. Add the Murray River pink salt a little at a time, checking for taste. Stir to incorporate, then freeze.

This recipe comes from New Zealand chef Jude Messenger, and works particularly well as an accompaniment to desserts such as sticky date pudding, treacle tart or anything that might be excessively sweet if served by itself.

Salted-butter Caramel Ice Cream

500 ml (17 fl oz) whole milk
300 g (10½ oz) sugar
4 tablespoons salted butter
½ teaspoon sea salt
250 ml (8½ fl oz) heavy cream
5 large egg yolks
¾ teaspoon vanilla extract
1 portion salted caramel (page 126)

Salted-butter Caramel Ice Cream

This ice cream uses the brittle caramel from page 126 to give a salty crunch to sweet, buttery caramel ice cream.

Caramelise the sugar the same way as for the salted caramel on page 126. Remove from the heat and stir in the butter and the salt. When the butter has melted, gradually whisk in the cream.

Set half the milk in a bowl over ice. Pour the other half into the caramel and set back on the heat. Whisk the egg yolks in a bowl, then pour a little of the hot caramel over the eggs. Pour the heated egg yolks back into the saucepan and cook, stirring constantly, until the mixture thickens.

Strain the custard through a fine sieve into the chilled milk, add the vanilla and stir frequently until the mixture cools. Freeze, then churn in an ice-cream maker. Break the salted caramel into small pieces and stir quickly through the churned ice cream.

fresh cream	
sea salt	

Butter

"Give me butter, butter and more butter", the great French chef, Fernand Point, would say. Because butter is one of the cornerstones of cooking. If you make your own, you will realise how much difference fresh butter makes. And you have the choice whether to leave it unsalted, in which case it will need to be used quickly, or to salt it.

Pour the cream into a mixing bowl and let it sit for about 12 hours so that it sours. Put the bowl in the mixer and start beating at a medium speed. Watch the process carefully. The cream will form stiff peaks, then begin to clump together. The clump will then suddenly release all of the buttermilk; be careful, as it may splash.

Pour the buttermilk into a container and save for later use (the recipe for *fromage blanc* on page 142 uses buttermilk). Continue whipping the butter for a few minutes until almost all of the liquid is released. Put the butter into some cheesecloth and squeeze under cold running water to remove the last of the buttermilk.

If you are leaving the butter unsalted, put it in the refrigerator and use within 3 or 4 days. Otherwise, take 2 or 3 pinches of sea salt and knead them into the butter. Store in a covered container.

❦

If you are going to make your own butter, you need to use the freshest cream you can get—it really is worth travelling to buy at the farm gate, particularly when you taste the results, spread over fresh homemade bread. And if you are leaving your butter unsalted, sprinkle a few flakes of fleur de sel or Cyprus black salt on your buttered bread to really make it sparkle.

Simple Cheese
1 kg (2¼ lb) plain, low-fat yoghurt
2 tablespoons fine sea salt

Simple Cheese

There is something almost mysterious about the process of turning milk into cheese. But it need not be so. All you need is milk—here in the form of yoghurt—and some salt. Time will do the rest.

Mix the salt into the yoghurt, then pour it into a large sieve or colander that has been lined with two layers of cheesecloth. Gather the edges of the cheesecloth and gently squeeze the yoghurt to expel some of the whey, then tie with string.

Hang the cheesecloth bag in a cool place, away from direct sunlight, with a container underneath to catch the whey. After 24–36 hours, when no more whey drips from the cheese, remove it from the bag and store, covered, in the refrigerator. It will keep for at least 10 days.

—

Use this simple cheese as you would cream cheese. The addition of fresh herbs will liven it up.

Fromage Blanc

1 l (2⅛ pints) very fresh whole milk
250 ml (8½ fl oz) heavy cream
500 ml (17 fl oz) fresh buttermilk
2 tablespoons lemon juice
½ teaspoon salt

Fromage Blanc

By its very nature, fresh fromage blanc is almost impossible to buy, because it doesn't travel well, being difficult to keep fresh for more than a day or two. So it stands to reason that you should make your own, particularly as the process is so simple, the results so versatile and delicious.

Mix the buttermilk and the lemon juice. Put the milk and the cream in a large, heavy saucepan and set over a very low heat. Add the buttermilk and take the mixture, very slowly, up to 90°C (194°F). While the milk is heating stir exactly twice, making two strokes each time with a spatula. As soon as the mixture reaches the required temperature, remove from the heat and allow to sit for 10 minutes. Curds will begin to form.

Line a large colander with two layers of fine cheesecloth and set over a bowl. Gently ladle the curds and whey into the colander and allow to drain. When most of the whey has drained, lift the edges of the cheesecloth and tie together with string. Hang over the bowl in a cool place until all the whey is gone and the fromage blanc has reached the desired consistency. Store in the refrigerator and use within a week, or marinate in oil and fresh herbs, in which case it will keep for up to 1 month.

Brined Feta

Cheese making takes time. It also takes a lot of milk, and because there are so many amazing cheeses to be sampled already, it might seem that making anything more complicated than fromage blanc is a little...redundant.

Making your own feta, however, is eminently practical—the process is simple, satisfying and a great introduction to the world of cheese making. You will need a couple of specialised ingredients, but these are readily available from health-food stores. You should be able to find pasteurised goat's milk in your supermarket.

Brined Feta

3.75 l (8 pints) whole pasteurised goat's milk
1¼ teaspoons mesophilic starter
1 teaspoon liquid calf's rennet
60 ml (2 fl oz) of cool water
4 tablespoons sea salt

Heat the goat's milk slowly over a double boiler until it reaches 29°C (84°F), then add the mesophilic starter. Blend with a whisk, remove from the heat, cover and let stand for 1 hour to ripen.

Mix the rennet with the water and stir into the ripened milk. Cover the pot for about 1 hour, allowing curds to form. Test the curd by cutting it with a knife: if no curd clings to the blade, it is ready.

Cut the curds into 2 cm (¾ in)cubes and allow to rest. The whey will rise from the curds. Stir the curds gently over the next 30 minutes to keep them separated and work off any extra whey. Ladle the curds into a colander lined with a double thickness of cheesecloth, tie the ends up to form a bag and hang in a cool place for approximately 5 hours.

If no more whey is dripping from the bag, and the curds feel as one firm, solid mass, transfer them to a large bowl. Cut the feta into 2-cm (¾-in) cubes and sprinkle liberally with the salt, ensuring all surfaces are covered.

Cover the bowl loosely with cling film and a tea towel and refrigerate for 5 days. The feta will then be ready to use. Transfer the cheese, along with the accompanying brine, into an airtight container and keep in the refrigerator until ready to serve.

❦

This is the entry point for true cheese making. If you wish to take it further, you will need to buy a cheese press or make one yourself. A simple cheese press can be made using a large round tin that has had its lid cleanly removed. Punch a few holes in the base of the tin, and find a plate of the same diameter, or cut a piece of plywood to fit. Then, all you need is a series of weights to gradually increase the pressure on the cheese as it ages.

Aged Cheese

5 l (10½ pints) whole milk	
1 l (2⅛ pints) additional cream (optional)	
5 ml (1 teaspoon) liquid starter or DVI dry starter (or ½ cup of live yoghurt/live buttermilk, although this is not as reliable as a commercial starter)	
3 ml (½ teaspoon) rennet	
10 g (⅜ oz) salt	

Aged Cheese

Making hard cheese is really not much more complicated than making feta—it is mainly a product of aging. The starter is available from health-food or specialty stores, and you will need an accurate thermometer. After that, all you need is time.

Cool the milk to 2°C (36°F). Stir in the starter and leave the milk, covered in a warm place for about an hour so that it can acidify.

On the stovetop, increase the temperature to 30°C (86°F). Mix the rennet with 2 teaspoonfuls of previously boiled and cooled water and then stir it in. Stir again 5 minutes later to stop the cream collecting at the top. Cover the container and then leave the milk to set in a warm place. The curd is normally ready when it is firm to the touch, gives slightly and does not leave a milk stain on the back of the finger.

Cut down into the curd, from top to bottom one way then cut it at right angles to form square columns. The curd is then loosened from around the walls of the pan. Make diagonal cuts to break the curd into pieces that are about pea-sized. Stir gently with the hand for a couple of minutes.

Gradually increase the temperature to 38°C (100°F) over the next 30–40 minutes, stirring occasionally. Give the whey a final, circular stir—the curds will gradually sink to the bottom. Turn off the heat and leave the pan until all movement has ceased in the liquid.

Ladle out as much of the liquid whey as possible, then place a previously sterilised cloth over a large container and tip in the curds. Make the cloth into a bundle by winding one corner around the other three. This is called a Stilton knot. Place the bundle on a tray which is tilted at an angle to let the whey drain away. Leave for about 15 minutes.

Untie the bundle and the curds will be seen to have formed into a mass. Cut this into four slices and place one on top of the other then cover with the cloth. After about 15 minutes place the outer slices of the curd on the inside of the stack, and vice versa. Repeat this process several times until the curd resembles the texture of cooked breast of chicken when it is broken open.

Cut the curd into pea-sized pieces and sprinkle the salt onto the curds, rolling them gently without breaking them further.

Line the mould from a cheese press with previously boiled cheesecloth and add the curd until the mould is full. Fold the corners of the cloth over the top of the cheese. Put the lid on the press, then weight down with a tin. After 1 hour, add another tin, until you have five in total.

Next day, remove the cheese from the press, replace the cloth with a clean one and put the cheese back in the mould, upside down, and press for another 24 hours. Remove the cheese from the press and cloth and dip it in hot water (66 °C [150°F]) for 1 minute in order to consolidate and smooth the surface. Place it in a protected area at a temperature of 18-21°C (64–70°F) and leave it to dry for a day or two until a rind begins to form. Once the rind has formed, the cheese can be sealed to prevent it

becoming unduly desiccated while it is maturing. Large cheeses are sometimes bandaged but it is much easier to use cheese wax that is available from specialist suppliers.

Using a water bath, heat the wax in a pan and stir it to ensure that it is melting evenly. Dip the cheese into the liquid wax and coat thoroughly.

Leave to mature in a cool, dry place at 8–11°C (46–51°F) where it should be turned daily for the first 3 weeks, then on alternate days after that. For a large mild cheese, ripening should take place for at least 3 months. A longer period of ripening produces a more mature cheese. Smaller cheeses are usually ready after a month.

the story of salt

From the Source

All salt comes from the sea—even salt that has been mined from high in the Himalayas, or evaporated from brine springs in inland Australia. In fact the world's largest salt flat, Salar de Uyuni in Bolivia, estimated to contain up to ten billion metric tons of salt, lies at a height of over 3,500 m (11,500 ft) above sea level. All of that salt was once suspended in the waters of a vast prehistoric lake. And that lake was once part of the sea.

Which is not to say that all salts are the same. The recipes in this book call for rock salt, sea salt and occasionally table salt. Each of these salts is noticeably different in the way it looks, feels and even tastes. The rock salt will have larger, harder crystals that are indeed similar to small rocks. The sea salt will be lighter, flakier, and its flavour will carry a hint of the various minerals it contains. The crystals of table salt will be much finer, more uniform and—somehow—saltier.

We have seen (page 43) how we can turn ordinary table salt into something that resembles natural sea salt, simply by dissolving it in water and then allowing the water to slowly evaporate in the sun. But it won't be sea salt.

Modern table salt is at least 95%—and sometimes as much as 99%—pure sodium chloride (NaCl). Of that, the proportions are almost exactly 40% sodium and 60% chloride. To this salt the manufacturers may have added iodine in the case of iodised salt, a small amount of sugar that prevents the loss of iodine and stops the salt yellowing, and probably an anti-caking agent such as calcium silicate or a compound of aluminium. All of the other minerals that are found naturally in seawater will have been removed in the refining process.

Seawater does not just contain sodium chloride. There are another 83 naturally occurring minerals to be found in the world's oceans: sodium chloride is simply the most numerous of them, comprising over 75% of the suspended solids.

Which is why seawater tastes salty, and why "natural" sea salt will contain not just sodium chloride but also magnesium, calcium, potassium, iron and iodine, along with trace amounts of a number of other minerals.

A Wealth of Salt

Depending on where you are, if you should dip a cup into the sea the water you scoop up will contain between 1% and 5% sodium chloride: the lesser figure if you are near the north or south pole, and the greater in any small, enclosed sea such as the Mediterranean.

The average salinity of seawater is therefore around 2.5%. If your cup had a capacity of 4 l (8½ pints), then on average the water you had scooped up would yield, after evaporation, approximately 105 g (3¾ oz) of salt. On a slightly different scale, if you evaporated 1 km³ (¼ m³) of seawater it would leave 26 t (28.5 t) of salt. And if you evaporated all of the world's oceans, the remaining salt would equal almost 15 times the mass of continental Europe.

The amounts are staggering, the supply of salt seemingly inexhaustible. Yet human history may be seen in one light as little more than the continuing quest for salt. If salt is indeed so plentiful, why has the finding and the extracting of it required so much effort and ingenuity? As Mark Kurlansky writes in *Salt: A World History*, likely to remain the definitive work on the subject, "for all of history until the twentieth century, salt was desperately searched for, traded for, and fought over. For millenia, salt represented wealth." Yet it is something that, again in Kurlansky's words, "fills the ocean, bubbles up from springs, forms crusts in lake beds, and thickly veins a large part of the earth's rock fairly close to the surface."

The reason is that the amount of salt that is easily accessible has never been enough to satisfy demand. People need salt, and as civilisation progressed, the need for salt progressed along with it.

This human requirement for salt can, presumably, be traced back to the successful transition of life from sea to land over 300 million years ago. For that transition to be successful, bodily cells had to be bathed in a salty solution similar to seawater.

But as life on land evolved—in hot humid climates and with a herbivorous diet—there was much less available salt. So we adapted a complex physiology to conserve body sodium, and developed an appetitive response to sodium in foods, encouraging us to consume foods that contained sodium. And these mechanisms, which developed over millions of years in a vastly different food environment, remain with us today.

Salt for Survival

The average salinity of blood and other intercellular fluids is around 0.9%, and the body of an average adult contains around 250 g (8¾ oz) of sodium chloride. Without it, quite simply, we would die, and as the body constantly loses salt through bodily functions, it must be replaced.

Sodium, a mineral that the body cannot manufacture for itself, is vital for transmitting electrical impulses through the nerves, assisting muscle contraction and controlling the distribution of water in the body. Chloride is essential for digestion, supplies the basis of the hydrochloric acid in the stomach's gastric juices, and enhances the ability of the blood to carry carbon dioxide from respiring tissues back to the lungs.

Sodium and chloride—along with a host of other elements, including zinc, iron, potassium and magnesium—are essential to both life and health. But the amounts are remarkably small: the Yanomamo indians of the Brazilian rainforest, famous for the miniscule amounts of salt they consume, reportedly survive on less than 0.5 g of salt per day. If that is all the human body needs to survive, then it does not quite explain why from the beginning of civilisation salt has been one of mankind's most sought-after commodities.

The simple answer is that salt preserves. It draws from food the moisture that would support bacteria, and is itself an antibacterial agent. Whether in curing meats or pickling or fermenting vegetables, salting was the predominant method of preserving food from before recorded history until the mid 1920s, when Clarence Birdseye perfected his technique of snap-freezing food and General Electric produced the first mass-market refrigerator.

It was, we might say, the beginning of a new ice age. It was also the end of salt as a necessary food preserver.

Since the end of the last great ice age, when people first domesticated animals, cultivated vegetables and learned to harvest the fields of wild grain that appeared in the wake of the retreating ice, our salt requirements have grown continuously. With a diet which was now largely vegetables and grains, and only occasionally the meat of domestic animals, men and women needed more salt to eat. They needed salt for their animals. And a farming rather than nomadic lifestyle, where food supplies are dictated by the seasons, required that provisions be stored so as to survive the scarcity of winter. Which in turn required more salt.

The great civilisations of Egypt and China were making salt on an industrial scale by the time recorded history began. The Egyptians evaporated seawater in the delta of the Nile; the Chinese were boiling brine in iron pans by around 450 B.C., and in 252 B.C. the first brine wells were drilled in Sichuan Province. In what is now Austria and Germany a race of Celts were using sophisticated mining techniques to obtain rock salt from mountain deposits, using the salt to cure meat, and travelling across vast distances of Europe, perhaps even as far as China, to trade their products.

These then are the three methods of salt production: solar evaporation, mining and mechanical evaporation, and the boiling of brine. Each method was in use long before history began, and though technological advances constantly improved efficiencies, the basic processes remained unchanged for millenia. In 1888, when the first vacuum-pan evaporater used to make salt was operating in New York, the great salt works of Cheshire in England were still using lead pans heated by coal fires to evaporate the brine—exactly the same way it had been done in Roman times.

overleaf Inca terraced salt pans, the Salineras de Maras, that have been in use for centuries.

The Means of Production

When the Romans first came to Britain around A.D. 43 they found native Britons who still made salt by the most primitive of methods, pouring brine on to hot charcoal and then scraping off the salt once it had cooled.

In contrast, the Chinese had by the same time been drilling brine wells for nearly 300 years, wells that in some cases reached 100 m (328 ft) deep. They had also made the discovery, unfortunate at first, that where there was salt there was also sometimes an invisible substance that inexplicably caused people to die. Occasionally it exploded. This substance was deemed to be an evil spirit, emerging from the ground in angry consternation at being disturbed. Offerings were made to placate it; and over time it came to be realised that the spirit could not only be tamed, it could even be put to work.

The invisible substance was natural gas, which along with oil is frequently found alongside salt deposits. Salt is impermeable, and where organic material has been trapped between salt and rock it eventually decomposes under the pressures of geology and time to become either oil or gas.

The Chinese soon learned to make use of this new resource. The same pipes that carried the brine from underground could also, if properly insulated, transport this invisible substance to where the brine was boiled. Instead of solid fuel, arduous to cut and difficult to transport, by around A.D. 200 they were cooking with gas.

Letting Nature Do the Work

It is less a cliché than a truism of history to say that necessity is the mother of invention. In inland China the oldest, simplest method for obtaining salt was never an option. For a start, it requires a coastline.

Solar evaporation has been used since it was first realised that salt crystals formed naturally at the edge of trapped pools of seawater. But it is practical on a large scale only in warm climates where the evaporation rate exceeds the rate of precipitation—a "negative evaporation rate"—by around 75 cm (29½ in) per year, at least for extended summer periods. If there are steady prevailing winds, so much the better.

The process itself could not be more simple. Saltwater is captured in shallow ponds and left to sit. When the sun and wind has evaporated a certain amount of water, and the brine has reached a certain concentration, it is moved to the next pool.

The concentration of the brine can be seen in the dramatic colours that are produced by varying concentrations of algae, brine shrimp and other pond life, making the ponds appear as if they have been dyed. These microorganisms change colour according to the salinity of their environment, thus the tint of each pond is an indication of its salinity. Low-salinity ponds proliferate with green algae, but in high-salinity ponds red algae are predominant. Millions of tiny brine shrimp can also cast an orange shade over ponds.

The series of concentrating ponds takes the brine from a concentration of 2.5% to a saturated solution of slightly more than 26%. The brine is then transferred to the final crystallising pond, where it reaches a specific gravity of 1.26. At this point, being 1.26 times more dense than water, the brine is oversaturated, and the salt begins to crystallise, sinking to the floor of the pond. The remaining brine, now a dark red and thick with magnesium, calcium and other minerals, is siphoned off.

By this stage the salt is essentially made, and is sitting in a waterless pond which may be as large as 1 sq km (⅜ sq m), its floor thick with salt from years of deposition, awaiting harvest. From there it will be pushed by bulldozers into huge mounds, then transferred for processing, where it will be washed first in a saturated brine, then in fresh water, mechanically dried and finally graded for packaging.

The salt ponds in San Francisco Bay produce around 700,000 t (772,000 t) of salt in this manner every year. In the south of France, in the vast delta known as the Camargue, the Rhone River empties into the Mediterranean. It is an area of nearly 1,000 sq km (386 sq m), made up of inland salt lakes, marshes and interconnecting waterways; sea salt is its most important harvest, and in the summer it may produce up to 15,000 t (16,535 t) per day. In contrast, only 25,000 t (27,580 t) per year are extracted from the Salar de Uyuni, the world's largest salt flat.

Indeed, so vast are some of the world's salt ponds they give lie to the idea the Great Wall of China is the only man-made structure that can be seen from space, and their patchwork of irregular, multi-coloured forms has often given both airline passengers and astronauts cause for wonder.

Cathedrals of Salt

Not all of the wonders of salt extraction are so visible. Like most inland people, the inhabitants of southern Poland got their salt from under the ground. For more than 4,500 years the ancient brine springs of the area had provided a readily accessible source, but the springs were not inexhaustible, and in the middle of the thirteenth century the people were forced to start digging. The brine had dried up, but the rock salt that for millenia had been its source was still there.

Salt miners dug for centuries, first as virtual slaves, then later as free men. The mines, at Wieliczka and Bochnia near Kraków, kept on getting deeper, producing a seemingly endless amount of salt. This salt, owned by the Polish Crown, is reported to have provided a third of its annual revenues. And, in order to keep such valuable workers happy, the mine operators began to offer, in 1689, underground religious services; the Catholic miners responded by carving first religious figures and then an entire chapel into the salt that surrounded them.

Throughout the ages salt has been mined by a method called "room and pillar", by which the salt is removed in a checkerboard pattern that leaves permanent, solid pillars as support for the mine roof. Anywhere from 45% to 65% of the salt is removed, leaving rooms that may be over 6 m (19¾ ft) high and with a floor that may be as large as a ballroom.

Which is what the workers of the Wieliczka mine created: ballrooms, dining rooms and even a series of lagoons. They carved freestanding statues, and they carved scenes in bas-relief into the walls, floors and ceilings. They dissolved the rock salt, refined and reconstituted it into clear, glass-like crystals, and from these they made chandeliers to light the rooms. It became an astonishing place, fit for royalty, and the Polish monarchs used the mine as a place to entertain themselves and visiting aristocracy, dancing in the ballrooms and boating on the underground lagoons.

But the hosting of royal parties did not prevent the mine from working, and it was only in 1996 that active mining was discontinued due to low salt prices and problems with flooding. The Bochnia mine remained open, and is now the world's oldest continuously operational salt mine.

The Wieliczka mine was made a UNESCO World Heritage Site in 1978, and now attracts over a million tourists each year. They come to marvel at Grand Hall, with its salt chandeliers, and the chapel's many intricate religious carvings, including a bas-relief representation of Da Vinci's *The Last Supper* and a statue of St Barbara, the patron saint of Poland.

Another small cause for wonder is that the salt out of which these things are carved is not white as it often appears in photographs, but rather varying shades of grey, so that it most resembles unpolished granite. This colour was a problem not just for Polish salt but for salt mined everywhere; the minerals with which it was coloured were not yet seen by consumers as being in any way desirable. The best salt was the whitest salt, and so that fetched the best prices.

Salt Mountains

Things have changed. It is no longer required that salt be pure white. Nor indeed that it be pure sodium chloride. The salt that lies in huge quantities in the mountainous areas of northern Pakistan and in the foothills of the Himalayas contains not only sodium chloride but also a further 84 trace elements—the same number as are found in the human body—including the iron, which accounts for its colour.

The salt has laid there for hundreds of millions of years. Legend claims that it was only discovered in 327 B.C. when Alexander the Great and his armies stopped on their march across the subcontinent. Reputedly, their battle-weary horses were seen to be licking the walls of caves in which they were sheltered, and curious soldiers followed suit. The rock was salty, the horses revived, and what was to become the second-largest salt mine in the world had been found.

The Khewra mine now produces around 325,000 t (350,250 t) of salt per annum. The salt ranges in colour from transparent to white, light and dark pink, through to the rich raw-beef colour of iron oxide. Because the salt has been underground for so long it is uncontaminated by toxins or pollutants; this purity, and the beauty of its colouration, has made pink salt from the Himalayas a sought-after commodity, justifying the great effort necessary to extract it from deep in the earth.

Because there are still much easier ways to get salt than to dig for it. All you really need is the sea, sunlight and time.

overleaf Aerial view of salt evaporation ponds in San Francisco Bay, USA—the tint of each pond is an indication of its salinity.

Raking in Profits

Sea salt, for centuries, was rarely referred to as sea salt. It was called Bay salt. The name comes from the Bay of Bourgneuf, situated on France's Atlantic coast between Guérande in the north and Ile de Ré in the south. Its saltworks had become so dominant in the production of solar evaporated sea salt that the name was soon generic. For consumers throughout Europe, all sea salt was Bay salt, whether it came from there or not.

Bay salt was not necessarily the *best* salt—other salts, such as those that came from Setúbal in Portugal, were whiter and therefore more pure, at least in the mind of the consumer. Bay salt could be green, grey or even black. But it was cheap, its crystals were large and there was plenty of it, which was a distinct advantage in an age when nearly all food still had to be cured, pickled or fermented in order for it to last. Households that were affluent enough could afford to buy a finer, whiter salt for the table. Those that were not so well off could always dissolve the Bay salt and then recrystallise it themselves, creating the equivalent of expensive table salt at much less cost.

But it was not the home market that drove the demand for Bay salt. The medieval Church, sexual passion and the eternal lust for profit saw to it that every year more and more salt was needed.

In the Middle Ages the Catholic Church was all-powerful, dictating virtually every aspect of the daily lives of the faithful, which in Europe was almost everybody. The power of the Church extended even to the table, and on religious days the eating of meat was forbidden.

There were many religious days: Fridays, the day on which Christ was crucified, the 40 days of Lent and various saint's days, were all considered "lean" days. All in all, this added up to nearly half of the year. Many activities were proscribed on these lean days, including sex. People were permitted only one meal. And because red meat was thought to inflame passions, it was not allowed—up until the time of Henry VIII one could still be hanged for the crime of eating meat on Friday.

Fortunately the animals that lived in water were seen to be "cool", and their flesh could be eaten without fear of arousal. The Church even condoned the consumption of sea otters—but only the tails. Porpoise and whale meat were permitted but were prohibitively expensive for most. Fish was, of course, the perfect compromise, still plentiful and cheap. It's only problem was that it did not travel well, and a large portion of the population lived inland.

The Fat of the Sea

It was probably the Egyptians who were the first to use salt for curing meat and fish—food preserved in such a way was left in ancient tombs, that the dead might have something to eat in the afterlife.

The salts they used were not pure sodium chloride, but also probably included saltpetre, which is a powerful antibacterial agent, and nitrites that directly inhibit the microorganism that causes botulism. With these, the salting of fish, naturally more difficult to preserve than meat, was made easier.

The Egyptians traded salt fish with the Phoenicians, who in turn learned the techniques themselves, providing them with another product for their famously large stock in trade. The Phoenicians also learned to catch the giant bluefin tuna that passed through the Mediterranean on their way to the Black Sea to spawn. And, it was the Phoenicians who founded the saltworks near Trapani in Sicily—famous today for the quality of its salt—so as to more easily cure their catch.

Like all of the great maritime peoples, the Phoenicians knew their fish. The Basques, who some speculate had sailed to America many years before Columbus, knew about not just fish but whales, which they had learned to hunt and kill, and whose meat they cured with salt. The Vikings, those fierce sea-borne raiders from the north, knew about cod, the fish whose life as bottom dwellers in the cold Atlantic waters means that their firm white flesh is almost entirely without fat.

Fat is the enemy of salt, at least when it comes to curing. It slows the rate of penetration, which is why most oily fish is packed in barrels to prolong contact with the salt; if left out in the air the fat will soon turn rancid.

The Vikings had little in the way of salt. But because of its lack of fat, they found that cod would keep well enough if dried in the cold, northern air. It became, along with the many slaves they captured in their raids, a profitable commodity, and by the ninth century their trading had taken them as far south as the Basque provinces. The Basques seem to have taken note of the Viking's superior ships, made of overlapping planks, and started building their own craft in the same style. They may also have tasted the Viking's air-dried cod.

Either way, within a generation of the encounter the Basques had made the journey north to the Faroe Islands, the Viking's home since they departed Scandinavia, and where the cold Atlantic waters were home to cod in their tens of millions. They already knew how to salt fish. But here was a fish, available in unfathomable numbers, which could be both dried and salted, thereby creating a food product that was virtually imperishable.

More Salt Needed

Along with introducing cod and advanced shipbuilding to the Basques, the Vikings may also have helped improve French saltmaking. Mark Kurlansky suggests that Viking settlement on the island of Noirmoutier in the Bay of Bourgneuf roughly coincides with the adoption of artificial pond techniques that greatly increased production. French historians, he notes, roundly reject such an idea.

What is irrefutable is that as cod grew in importance, so did Bay salt, which was thought to be the only type suitable for curing fish. Salt cod was an extremely resilient foodstuff, as hard as a plank of wood, and able to be stacked and shipped virtually anywhere, even to the heated climates of Spain. But once it had been soaked overnight in fresh water the result was at least comparable to fresh, church-approved fish. It could sustain not just the mass of believers but also armies and navies; one of the first preparations for war was always to obtain a large quantity of salt, meat and fish.

How important was salt fish? So important that by the eighteenth century the salt intake of the average European was an astonishing 70 g (2⅜ oz) a day, the bulk of which came from salt fish.

Salt production had to keep up—there were profits to be made—and it had to do so without technology and without mechanisation. Whether improved by Viking know-how or not, the inland sea around Guérande came to contain almost 1,820 ha

(4,500 acres) of salt ponds that were worked by the paludiers, a name that literally translates as "swamp workers".

Each worker had his own pond or ponds, fed by the tides through a series of channels and separated from these channels by wooden dams. These dams had holes in them at various heights, stoppered by plugs, and the paludier could alter the water level of his ponds by unplugging the appropriate hole. When the waters reached saturation point, and crystals began to form, the paludier used a wooden rake held at the end of a long pole to scrape the salt into piles. This is the salt that was once called Bay salt but has come to be known as sel gris, grey salt, from the colour obtained from the dense clay floor, or *argile*, of the salt ponds.

The paludier's work was a skilled craft, belying the origins of the name: his feel for the harvest had to be such that the salt came out at the right colour, size and consistency every time. Even so, he was not considered deft enough to harvest the fleur de sel, the flower of salt, which was, and is, the most prized salt of all.

Salt crystals, being more dense than water, will almost always sink. But in the summer months of the harvest season the hot dry winds that blow over the shallow ponds cause salt crystals to precipitate that are larger, flakier, and therefore lighter. These delicate flakes sit on the surface of the pond, and at the end of each day they are gathered with a *lousse à de fleur*, a wooden board attached to a pole that skims the surface just enough to dislodge the fleur de sel. Only women were permitted to use the lousse à de fleur, because only a woman's hand was considered delicate enough to gather the salt without damaging the precious flakes.

Strangely, women were not considered too delicate to then carry large bowls of fleur de sel, weighing up to 30 kg (66 lb), along the maze of narrow paths between the ponds to where the salt was packaged.

Five hundred years later, virtually nothing has changed: the work is no longer restricted to women, and there are wheelbarrows to transport the salt across the narrow dikes. Otherwise, the methods are the same. Each pond produces one batch of fleur de sel per day, usually about 1 kg (2¼ lb), and this salt, with a record of its provenance attached, will go on to grace upmarket tables around the world, at a cost of more than ten times the grey salt on top of which it sits.

overleaf Man raking sel gris in the Guérande marshes, Pays de la Loire, France.

That Salty Taste

It is not just sugar that tastes sweet: honey, maple syrup, fruit and a host of artificial sweeteners do the job equally well. Many things are sour or bitter. But only one thing is salty.

Yet that thing, strictly speaking, is not salt.

We must remember that what we call salt is almost always shorthand for sodium chloride. Its two elements, sodium and chlorine, are joined together by an ionic bond, whereby the sodium atom loses an electron, which the chlorine atom gains. This shared atom bonds the two together to form sodium chloride, or NaCl, whose molecules form a lattice structure. This structure is isometric, equal along all three axes, so the molecules of sodium chloride are formed in a perfect cube.

They are also soluble in water, as is any molecule with an ionic bond, and when added to food or put straight in the mouth, the sodium and the chloride will quickly separate again. The chloride will taste of nothing, because the tongue has no receptors to bind with it. But evolution has created for us a unique, sodium-specific taste transduction mechanism on the taste receptor cells. So when sodium hits our tongue, it tastes...salty.

We have already noted that the primary function of the sense of taste is checking the quality of food to be ingested—and that the sense of pleasure taste gives us is merely a fortunate by-product of this function.

A Taste for Pleasure

The majority of taste receptor cells are organized into rosette-like structures called taste buds, which are embedded in papillae on the tongue. And as all schoolchildren know, the taste buds are sensitive to different things, depending on where they are located: the tip of the tongue is sensitive to sweet, the back of the tongue sensitive to bitter and the sides to sour and salty.

Except this is not really true. The tip of the tongue may be slightly more sensitive to sweet, but it still perceives all the other tastes, including umami or "meatiness", now widely considered the "fifth taste". All we need to do to confirm this is dip the tip of the tongue into any substance. Certainly we will be able to taste what it is.

Here's how the tasting mechanism works: when a tastant (a molecule that transmits taste) binds with receptors or ion channels in the membrane of a papillary sensory cell within a taste bud, the electrical potential of the cell is modified as a result of a series of reactions. The cell commences to excite neurons which, little by little, convey information to the brain.

This will not, however, give us the full story. Given that there are but five basic taste qualities, the immense diversity of flavours we associate with food are primarily derived from the sense of smell. When food or liquids are chewed and swallowed, volatile compounds are released into the oral cavity. These volatile compound activate receptors located high in the nasal cavity.

So flavour is usually a single perception derived from the senses of both taste and smell. In the words of Dr Russell Keast, Senior Lecturer in Sensory Science at Deakin University in Melbourne, Australia, "The experience of flavour begins with the stimulation of numerous chemical/physical receptors within the senses of taste and smell, which are influenced by the food matrix, mastication, saliva, food temperature, and the internal state of the observer. During the process of eating, additional sensory and cognitive interactions within and among these modalities can influence the perceived flavour of a food."

The Appliance of Science

One of these modalities is of course salt. The famous French food chemist and writer, Hervé This, writes in *Molecular Gastronomy: Exploring the Science of Flavour*, that "without salt, agreeable tastes forfeit their prominence, and they are unable to prevent disagreeable tastes from asserting themselves."

Hervé This reports that researchers at the Monell Chemical Senses Institute in Philadelphia, USA have found that "sodium ions selectively suppress bitterness (and probably other disagreeable tastes as well) while intensifying agreeable tastes."

With regards to taste, salt has another, equally important property: its chemical structure means that it increases the ionic strength of aqueous solutions. This makes it easier for odorant molecules to separate themselves from food, and it explains why foods that are largely water—soup, for example—are relatively tasteless unless well salted.

And soup is a perfect example of the fact that we rarely consume food which possesses only one taste: most food is a complex mixture of many flavour-eliciting chemicals. Which means that salt has multiple routes by which to influence flavour, aside from the direct path of just adding saltiness.

For example, according to Dr Keast, the bitter-suppressing effect of the sodium ion is due to its chemical properties acting on taste transduction mechanisms, rather than the actual perceived taste of salt. When one compound that tastes bitter is mixed with another compound that tastes sweet, the resulting mixture is often a combination of the two tastes—a bitter-sweet solution—but the intensity of the mixture is less than the sum of the intensity of its components. This phenomenon is known as mixture suppression. And if the bitterness of the bitter-sweet mixture is suppressed by salt, then the intensity of the sweetness is enhanced, because more sweetness is released from the mixture suppression.

Another factor we must take into account is the enhancement of congruent flavours. When sweetness is released from mixture suppression, the increased sweetness also increases the perceived intensity of congruent or similar flavours. For example, we may have a raspberry-flavoured food that has some bitterness associated with it. The addition of salt to suppress the bitterness (but in a low enough concentration so as not to be salty) results in an increased sweetness, and the increased sweetness in turn enhances the congruent raspberry flavour. There is no actual change in raspberry flavour; but when the brain processes the signals an enhancement is perceived. As far as the brain is aware, it just tastes…better.

Something to Chew On

Chewing is essential. Besides imparting pleasure and satisfaction, it breaks down the food matrix, adjusts its temperature to that of the body, and releases flavour-eliciting compounds that stimulate the senses. The physical property of the food matrix as well as the efficiency of chewing determines the speed of food breakdown, and thus the extent of flavour release.

The physical processes that occur during eating—saliva flow, mastication and swallowing—are important in determining the release rate of sodium to the taste receptor cells. We notice the difference, for example, between chewing bread and drinking soup. Despite the high concentration of sodium in much of our bread, the intensity of its saltiness will not be as strong. The structural matrix of bread, its physical construction (and particularly the gluten matrix) limits the release of sodium, thereby slowing the activation of taste receptor cells. But if an equal concentration of sodium were added to water, the free availability of sodium to taste receptors would render it undrinkable.

And this is a problem. Around 75% of the sodium we consume comes from processed food. Much of the sodium added to processed food is invisible to our taste receptors as it remains bound in the food matrix. Only when the food is swallowed and then digested is the sodium released from the food matrix into the body.

It is commonly believed that we eat too much salt, and that excess sodium leads to the development of hypertension and subsequent diet-related diseases. Certainly it has been proven that a reduction of sodium in the diet will result in a concomitant reduction in blood pressure. But how much salt, really, is too much?

overleaf Coloured scanning electron micrograph of a grain of kosher salt.

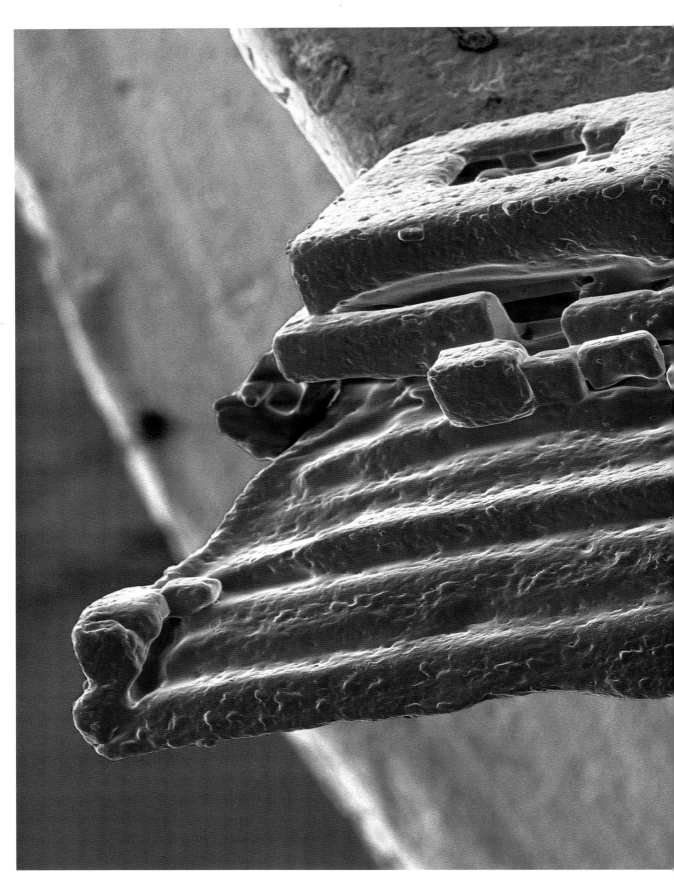

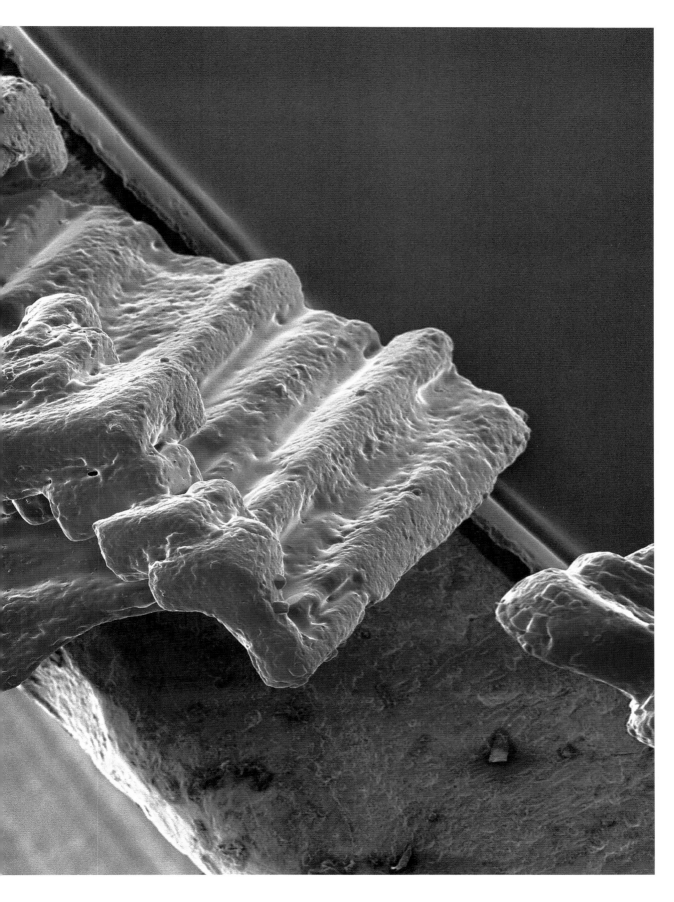

Saucy

The ancient Romans called it *garum*. In modern Southeast Asia it is variously called *nuoc mam* in Vietnam, *patis* in the Philippines, *budu* or *kecap ikan* in Malaysia and *nam pla* in Thailand. In English it is simply fish sauce.

Whatever name it might go by, it represents another of salt's many paradoxes. For what could possibly be more unappetising, indeed more potentially poisonous, than rotting fish? Yet the reality is that fermented sauces are one of the world's great staples, and that they would not be edible—or even possible—without salt.

The Romans made their garum with fish scraps. The innards, gills and tails, along with any fish that were too small to be cured, were placed in earthenware jars, layered with salt, weighted down and then left in the sun to ferment.

Before long, the action of the salt began to draw moisture from the fish. The jars were shaken, the fish released more liquid, and when no more was forthcoming the liquid was strained off. It then had to be tested to ensure it was sufficiently salty, using the age-old means of floating an egg in it. The sauce could then be used straight away by boiling it, adding some unfermented wine and carefully filtering the result. Or it could be left in the sun to ferment further.

The result was an expensive, powerful concoction that was certainly not to everyone's taste. Pliny, the Roman historian, referred to it as "that liquid of putrefying matter". Yet it was used not just as a condiment but as medicine, being prescribed for ailments as diverse as migraines and tuberculosis, as well as being applied as a topical ointment for sores.

As the Roman Empire declined, the making of garum in the West declined with it: most Europeans were of the opinion that leaving fish guts to rot in the sun was, in the words of Mark Kurlansky, "just one of those unpleasant hedonistic excess for which Rome was remembered", rather than a tradition they were inclined to keep.

But in Southeast Asia, and particularly Vietnam, where it is thought that the techniques of making fish sauce arose independently at around the same time, the tradition prospered. Today, with its various names, fish sauce is made in virtually every Asian country, even India, and remains, along with soy sauce, the primary medium by which Asian cuisine derives its salt.

Fortunately, unlike garum, Asian fish sauces were made not from scraps but small, whole fish. The only other ingredient was salt, which prevented the fish from rotting long enough for fermentation to begin. The same ingredients are still used today: a bottle of nam pla from Thailand, chosen at random from the supermarket shelf, shows that the ingredients are anchovies (68%), salt and sugar. A note on the label warns that "Salt crystals can occur naturally in high-quality fish sauce." The nutrition information panel shows that each 15 ml (½ fl oz) serving—one tablespoon—contains 1,186.8 mg of sodium. And by applying the National Heart Foundation of Australia's equation, we can calculate that each serving contains 2.967 g of salt. That's three-quarters of a teaspoon of salt for every tablespoon of sauce.

The Wonder Bean

In modern China, schoolchildren still learn a mnemonic jingle from the Middle Ages to help them remember the seven fundamental necessities of life. These are firewood, rice, oil, salt, soy sauce, vinegar and tea.

The soya bean must be regarded as the world's most versatile legume: from it man has learned to make oil, milk, curd (tofu), pastes (miso), sauces and even soymilk skin. Soy has twice the protein content of other legumes, and a balance of amino acids that is almost perfect for humans. But it is not the soya bean that Chinese schoolchildren have on their list of essentials, nor any of the other products created from it. It is soy sauce, the universal condiment in both China and Japan.

Soy sauce was originally a paste, made from cooked beans that had been treated with the *Aspergillus oryzae* mould and then immersed in brine, called *dou jiang* in China and miso in Japan. Sometimes, if this paste was made with excess liquid, there was a resulting residue. It was delicious (several hundred aroma molecules have been identified in soy sauce) and by around the year 1000 it was being prepared for its own sake. By the Middle Ages, as we have seen, it was one of the necessities of life.

Traditional fermented soy sauce contains between 8% and 15% salt. Modern "chemical" soy sauce, made with the residue from soya bean oil production that is then treated with hydrochloric acid and sodium carbonate, is saltier still, and may contain up to 2.5 g of salt per tablespoon.

The Essence of Flavour

It is no surprise then that traditional Chinese cuisine was not often seasoned by adding salt directly to food: along with soy sauce there are a number of other salty, fermented condiments, including monosodium glutamate (MSG), that they preferred to use.

Originally, monosodium glutamate came naturally in the form of a seaweed known as *konbu*, from which the Japanese made stock. It was isolated in 1908 by a Japanese chemist, Kikunae Ikeda, and scarcely a year later it was being manufactured commercially from wheat gluten proteins. It caught on rapidly, and soon came to be used in large quantities in both Japanese and Chinese kitchens. And although MSG is not a salt, like salt it contains sodium, as the name suggests, and acts as a flavour enhancer as well as having a specific taste of its own. Indeed, in China monosodium glutamate is called *wei jing*, "the essence of flavour".

The Chinese had spent millennia learning about flavour—their cuisine is essentially a balancing act of tastes set against each other, following the Taoist concept of yin and yang that was developed in the fourth century B.C. Saltiness was the fulcrum they used to balance the other five flavours—hot, sour, spicy, bitter and sweet—that make up Chinese cuisine. It was particularly believed to bring out sweetness and moderate sourness. Indeed saltiness is implicit in all Asian cuisine: without sauces such as hoisin, oyster sauce, nuoc mam and soy sauce it is virtually unimaginable.

Of Anchovies and Elephants

There is a sauce without which many modern Western foods (it would be a stretch to call them cuisine) might also be unimaginable. That sauce is ketchup, and it too would not exist without salt.

The name ketchup is a transliteration of the Indonesian *kecap*, a generic term for a fermented soy sauce which might become *kecap manis* if sweetened or *kecap ikan* if fermented with fish. The original ketchups gained their inspiration from such Asian sauces, but their roots were firmly Roman.

Although garum had essentially passed into history, it had a successor: the anchovy. Instead of having its innards fermented, the anchovy was gutted and salted whole, and by the seventeenth century had become enormously popular, due to its remarkably full flavour. And in an ironic development, the English discovered that these salted anchovies, if given a little heat and some liquid, would soon melt into a delicious sauce. "When this sauce has been made well, it would make you eat an elephant", the great gourmand Grimod de La Reynière enthused.

How a sauce of melted anchovies became a sweet-sour tomato condiment is a long process of evolution and changing tastes: over time a ketchup might have been based on walnuts, mushrooms or even lemons. It took an American to create the first recipe, some time prior to 1782, for "tomato ketchup". Soon it was an idea whose time had come. But, in another irony, of all the salt- and preservative-laden processed foods, ketchup has become far less salty—a randomly sampled product shows a salt content of just ⅓ teaspoon of salt per tablespoon of sauce.

overleaf Ruins of an ancient garum
factory near Tarifa, Andalusia, Spain.

Of Cabbages and Ham

It is interesting to note that every region, every people, has one food or dish that they seem to love above all others. It is even more interesting to observe that in so many places that dish is either cured meat or fermented cabbage. And in the case of Alsace and Lorraine, a region now divided between France, Germany and Switzerland, it is both.

The dish is called *choucroute garnie à l'Alsacienne*, a combination of sauerkraut and pork products that features on every restaurant menu in Alsace, and has been called by at least one gourmand a "dizzying, almost inconceivable gastronomic summit". Which is high praise for something whose principle ingredient is "sour grass".

Although it is now most closely linked with the German lands, fermented sliced cabbage has been a part of life in the Far East for thousands of years—the Chinese labourers who toiled on the Great Wall subsisted largely on sauerkraut. But theirs was fermented in rice wine, whereas the German version depends on salt.

The idea of fermented cabbage seems to have travelled east with the migrations of Central Asian tribes and the armies of Genghis Khan. Certainly the French, loath to acknowledge the German roots of anything that might be found in their own culture, attributed its origins to the Chinese. But its popularity in central and northern Europe was undeniable: cabbages were easy to grow, preserving them was equally straightforward, and the end result was particularly rich in vitamin C, which was invaluable during long northern winters when fruit and other vegetables were scarce.

The Alsatian word for it was *surkrut*, and by the sixteenth century there existed in Alsace the trade of *surkrutschneider*, literally "sauerkraut cutter". Each had his own jealously guarded recipe, which would include spices such as anise, cloves and cumin, along with horseradish, fennel, bay leaves and elderberries. The process itself was simple: layer chopped cabbage in a barrel, sprinkle with the accompanying spices, then cover with salt. Repeat. When the barrel is full a lid is put on and weighed down. The salt then draws water from the cabbage, which rises over the lid and seals the whole process from the air and any further bacteria. After a month the sauerkraut, or choucroute in French, is ready.

To serve choucroute garnie à l'Alsacienne in its most essential form, all one needs is a large platter of sauerkraut, and then some smoked bacon, salted bacon, smoked or salted pig's knuckles, three or four different types of sausage and a salted loin of pork to garnish. Simple.

More Pork

Legend has it that, some time long ago, a hunter wounded a wild boar and chased it into the marsh country around Salies-de-Béarn, a few miles north of the Basque lands in southern France, and by the time he found the animal lying in the water it was already preserved with salt. It is one of those legends that appears in different places in almost identical form, and the town hall of Lüneburg in Germany hangs an ancient ham, supposedly retrieved from nearby brine springs under precisely the same circumstances.

Neither the Basques nor Germans should claim the honour of making the first ham, such as we would recognise it today. For it was the Celts, fierce warriors and master salt-miners, whose ham came first. Salted meat was their specialty, and though they left no recorded history of their own, the Greeks and Romans documented their love of pork products.

The Romans adopted that passion. And the way in which they made ham was virtually the same as making sauerkraut, insofar as it was largely a matter of adding salt to the principal ingredient.

Cato, whose work *De Agricultura* is the oldest surviving complete book of Latin prose, gives a recipe that involves packing the hams one atop the other in a tub, each one completely separated by salt. "When the hams have been in salt five days, take them all out with the salt and repack them, putting those which were on top at the bottom…After the twelfth day remove the hams, brush off the salt, and hang them for two days in the wind. On the third day wipe them off clean with a sponge and rub them with oil. Then hang them in smoke for two days, and on the third day rub them with a mixture of vinegar and oil."

After that, he says, they may be hung in the meat house, "and neither bats nor worms will touch them".

The process of curing is really as simple as the procedure: Harold McGee, in his book *On Food and Cooking*, explains it in these terms. "The addition of salt—sodium chloride—to meat creates such a high concentration of dissolved sodium and chlorine ions outside the microbes that water inside their cells is drawn out, salt is drawn in, and their cellular machinery is disrupted. The microbes either die or slow down drastically. The muscle cells too are partly dehydrated and absorb salt."

For microbes, as for all things, without water there is no life. This fact is well illustrated by the process of fermentation, which brings sauerkraut into existence.

Plants contain certain benign microbes that, in the right conditions, will flourish, and in so doing will suppress the activities of other microbes, the ones that cause spoilage and disease. This they do by being the first to consume the plant's natural sugars. They convert these sugars to carbon dioxide, alcohol and lactic and other acids, all of which are hazardous to the "bad" microbes. The process also generates lactic acid bacteria, which add significant amounts of B vitamins, along with new, volatile substances that enrich the food's aroma.

There is perhaps a better way to sum up the magic of fermentation. The Koreans have a legend in which a poor farmer puts some withered old cabbages in a bowl of seawater to revivify them. When he looks at them a couple of hours later, he is overjoyed to discover they have swollen magnificently. This is matched by his disappointment the next day when he returns to find them limp and even smaller than they were to begin with. But there is a consolation, because they taste delicious.

The Salt Factor

Without salt, neither curing, fermenting or indeed cheesemaking would be possible. And because these processes have been man's primary methods of preserving food for maybe 7,000 years, it is no exaggeration to say that without them civilisation as we know it would have been impossible—without preservation techniques, agriculture on any scale is a pointless exercise, and without agriculture mankind would have remained as nomadic hunter-gatherers.

We are reminded of this every day. The eightieth birthday celebrations of the great French chef, Paul Bocuse, considered by many as the most important chef in modern cooking, were catered by the créme de la créme of international chefs. But Bocuse chose to eat a simple plate of *jamón Ibérico*, the Spanish ham considered one of the world's great culinary products. For him, there is no finer food.

The traditions of curing meat and fermenting cabbage run in an unbroken line for thousands of years. These techniques have been perfected over that time; the results are in the kimchee which for Koreans is essential to life, the choucroute garnie à l'Alsacienne and the jamón Ibérico, the Parmesan and Roquefort and Stilton cheeses whose tastes and textures are unequalled, the soy sauce that flavours virtually all Chinese food. All of these are a living link with history, and all of them owe their existence to salt.

overleaf Salting roquefort cheese, Roquefort, Aveyron, France.

Bread and Cheese

According to Harold McGee, it is one of the great achievements of humankind. The American writer, Clifton Fadiman, called it "milk's leap towards immortality". We call it cheese.

But why should cheese be so exalted? Certainly its origins are not promising: it is hard to imagine that curdled milk might be called one of the pinnacles of human achievement. Yet with the addition of two simple ingredients, salt and time, that is what it has become.

As with so many of civilisation's great developments, the first real evidence of cheesemaking comes from the Egyptians: residue from the process has been found in a pot dated 2300 B.C. The technique, of course, was by then thousands of years old. It is assumed to have been discovered in the Middle East or Central Asia around 5000 B.C., when people who had already noted the preserving power of salt applied that process to the curds of naturally soured milk. They also discovered that those curds were easier to work with if they had been formed in contact with the stomach of an animal.

And they needed a lot of salt, given the climate: milk is a particularly volatile substance, quick to spoil in any kind of heat, and the original purpose of cheese was of course to preserve milk for later use.

So, ancient cheeses were no doubt heavily salted, and may have resembled a modern brine-cured feta. But as the technique spread west and north, where temperatures grew cooler, less salt was required, and cheese would keep for longer. The microbes and their enzymes that still resided within it came, over time, to change the nature of cheese.

"In a sense, cheese came to life. It became capable of pronounced development and change; it entered the cyclical world of birth, maturation, and decline."

Thus Harold McGee captures the essence of cheese: it is alive.

And life brings diversity. The astonishing variety of cheeses comes from the fact that cheese, like any living thing, is a product of its environment. So many different elements contribute to the end result that cheese can seem to have a near infinite number of permutations; from cottage cheese to pecorino, feta to Gouda, gorgonzola to mozzarella.

The nature of the milk, the type of microbes, the cheesemaking process, the amount of salt and how long the cheese is aged for are only the most important elements determining the end result. The god of cheese is in the details.

The Creation Myth

In virtually every culture, we can gauge how important something is by whether it has a story. Like cured ham and pickled cabbage, cheeses too have a story.

One such tale is of a shepherd boy from a small village in a mountainous region of France, who absent-mindedly left his lunch of rye bread and cheese curd in one of the local caves. He returned a few weeks later to find that his lunch was still there. But it had undergone a transformation, and both the bread and the cheese curd were mouldy. The bread was inedible, but the cheese…

The cheese had become Roquefort, named for the village of Roquefort-sur-Soulzon that is located atop the system of caves in which the cheese is still ripened to this day. It is one of the world's great cheeses, and has been so since the Middle Ages. In 1411, King Charles VI gave rights to the ageing of Roquefort to only this village. It is produced by allowing a bread made from wheat and rye to go mouldy in the cool, damp caves. When the bread has turned blue it is ground into dust, which carries the spores of the mould *Penicillium roqueforti*, and these are sprinkled into the cheese. Once the wheels have been formed, they are rubbed with salt once, turned and rubbed with salt again and then set in the caves to age. A minimum of four months later, a cheese is born.

And it is probable that at least one of those cheeses may then complete the circle, finding its way, along with a piece of rye bread, into the lunchbox of a young sheep herder. Because for many people, even today, lunch is bread and cheese. It is one of those perfect combinations which, once settled upon, never change. Add a slice of ham and some pickles and you have a meal fit for a king.

Bread. Cheese. Pickles. Ham. We might be tempted to say that without salt none of these would be possible. But bread is the one thing that can be made perfectly well without salt. Granted, it won't be as good, but of all the major processes humankind has developed to transform or preserve food, the making of bread is the only one for which salt is not a true necessity.

Bread and Salt

Almost all bread is made with salt. It improves both the taste and the texture, and in sourdoughs helps limit the actions of the souring bacteria. Salt in bread made with yeast moderates the action of the yeast and allows it to produce carbon dioxide at a reasonable rate, resulting in a finer textured bread with small to medium air cells. This in turn allows for the flavour of the yeast to develop, as well as enhancing it. Salt also adds structure to the dough by strengthening the gluten, which keeps the carbon dioxide bubbles from expanding too rapidly.

Omitting or reducing the amount of salt can cause the dough to rise too quickly, adversely affecting the shape and flavour of bread—breads without salt tend to have paler crusts and a flat, dull taste.

So you can make bread without salt. But why would you? Like almost everything else we eat, bread is improved by salt. And of course it is not just our food; many of the industrial processes that have made an immeasurable difference to human life have salt as one of their essential ingredients—the tanning of leather, smelting of metal, glazing of pottery, and the making of soap, glass and gunpowder all require salt.

In fact, the figure commonly cited by the salt industry is around 14,000 separate and distinct uses for salt. By this estimation, salt would have to be acclaimed as possibly the most useful substance on our planet.

Certainly salt holds a place in human culture that is rivalled by few other items. Mark Kurlansky quotes the Welsh Jungian psychologist Ernest Jones, writing in the early twentieth century about the human obsession with salt, how "in all ages salt has been invested with a significance far exceeding that inherent in its natural properties, interesting and important as these are. Homer calls it a divine substance, Plato describes it as especially dear to the Gods, and we shall presently note that importance attached to it in religious ceremonies, covenants and magical charms. That this should have been so in all parts of the world and in all times shows that we are dealing with a general human tendency and not with any local custom, circumstance or notion."

Indeed, salt is as universal as bread, or wine, both as things in themselves and as symbols of some greater concept. But only salt seems to have the remarkable capacity of being all things to all people.

"Trust no one," the Roman statesman Cicero said, "until you have eaten much salt with him." He chose his words with care. Salt was so important to Rome and its people that many of the most fundamental underpinnings of their civilisation were described with reference to it.

And not just Rome. Throughout history, there have been no "civilisations" for whom salt was not a precious commodity, a means of exchange, a religious signifier, and a method of social and political control. In the words of author Margaret Visser, salt has "fascinated man for thousands of years not only as a substance he prized and was willing to labour to obtain, but also as a generator of poetic and of mythic meaning. The contradictions it embodies only intensify its power and its links with experience of the sacred."

The truth of this fact is not hard to verify. Because everywhere we look, if we look hard enough, we will see salt.

overleaf Hotel built with salt blocks at the edge of the Salar de Uyuni, Bolivian plateau, Bolivia.

The Wisdom of Salt

It is impossible to overstate the impact that salt has had on culture. The evidence is everywhere we look: in art, technology, religion, language and place names.

Take the word sauce. Or sausage. Salami. Salad. Salary. Salacious. Salubrious. They are of course all from the same root, *sal*, the Latin word for salt. Salacious is from *salax*, a "salted state", which was used to describe a man in love. The word salubrious is derived from *salus*, Latin for health—the root of which is plain.

Obviously the Romans felt strongly about salt. They used it to invoke and propitiate their gods. They built roads to transport it. The government taxed it to fund military campaigns, and they subsidised it to garner popular support. Salt was used to cure olives and to bind agreements. After their victory over the Phoenicians at Carthage they ploughed salt into the ground so that nothing would grow.

What the Romans knew is that salt is not always benign. It is estimated that in Australia an area the size of a football field is lost to salinity every hour, making the land impossible to farm. The fact that salt makes the earth barren, and in high enough concentration makes water undrinkable, means that salt has come to represent both life and death. In the Old Testament, when King Abimelech destroyed the city of Shechem he is said to have "sowed salt on it", a phrase expressing the completeness of its ruin. Yet in 2 Kings the Lord casts salt upon the waters, saying "I have healed these waters; there shall not be from thence any more death or barren land."

Destruction and healing; salt, this contradictory substance, may be responsible for both. Jesus calls his followers "the salt of the earth". The apostle Paul exhorts Christians to "let your conversation always be full of grace, seasoned with salt". And Jesus famously asks: "If the salt have lost his savour, wherewith shall it be seasoned?"

It seems as though salt may be all things to all people. In the Shinto ceremony of sumo, as much a religious rite as it is a sporting event, the circle is purified with salt before the wrestlers begin. A Buddhist monk throws salts to cleanse or purify the way at the start of a fire-walking ceremony that heralds the coming of spring. A witch consecrates water and salt at the beginning of a Wiccan ritual. At Passover seder Jews dip potatoes into saltwater, symbolising the tears shed by Hebrew slaves in Egypt. The Catholic Church dispenses holy salt, *Sal Sapientia*, the salt of wisdom.

The Name of the Place

The suffix "wich" at the end of English place names indicates that it was a place where salt was made. The name of Salzburg in Austria literally means "salt fortress". The province of Galicia in Spain and the Roman name for what was to become modern France—Gaul—are both rooted in the word for salt. Salsamaggiore, a town in Italy, means "big salt place".

If you look at a road map of America, the major cities are connected by the long, straight interstate highways built by President Eisenhower after World War II so that the transport of military equipment would be quicker and easier. In contrast, the secondary roads are a jumbled web that seem to conform to no sensible order.

But in reality they follow a profoundly logical pattern. Before the coming of the European, when North America was a vast, underpopulated wilderness, its animal inhabitants created paths to any naturally occurring source of salt. Native Americans followed these tracks, as did white explorers. Towns were established beside the salt, and the animal tracks became the roads that connected the towns.

Like harbours, rivermouths and lakeshores, saltworks were natural places to establish settlements. Rome itself was built, not (as legend suggests) on the site where a she-wolf suckled the twins Romulus and Remus, but rather in the hills behind a saltworks on the banks of the Tiber River. Most Italian cities were also founded near salt. The very first of the great Roman roads was the Via Salaria, the Salt Road.

The Romans needed salt to run their empire. The army, which expanded and maintained Roman control over its foreign conquests, needed salt for its soldiers, its horses and its livestock. Everyone knows that the word salary comes from the fact that Roman soldiers were paid in salt. But it is just as frequently claimed that the term refers to an allowance paid them in order to buy salt.

It is another example of the contradictory nature of this fascinating substance; necessary to life, but sometimes fatal. At over 450 pages, Mark Kurlansky's book *Salt: A World History* is a vast store of information about salt through the ages, including the fact that in "the most authoritative book of Jewish law, the *Shulchan Arukh* (The Prepared Table), written in the sixteenth century, it is explained that salt can only safely be handled with the middle two fingers. If a man uses his thumb in serving salt, his children will die, his little finger will cause poverty, and use of the index finger will cause him to become a murderer."

Bad Luck

In Leonard da Vinci's painting *The Last Supper*, Judas is shown spilling the salt. This has always been bad luck, down through the ages. Yet deliberately throwing more salt over one's left shoulder immediately afterwards will counter the mistake; the malevolent spirits that have appeared behind you will be driven away by the salt you throw. Tradition says that one should do the same when entering the house after a funeral.

The bringing of bread and salt into new houses is a longstanding tradition. The use of salt to protect newborn babies from harm was a feature of Jewish, Muslim and Christian practice. The practice of invoking the gods with salty water, originally pagan, was adopted by the Romans and then evolved into the Holy Water used by the Catholic Church. Baptism, too, was originally done in salty water.

So salt was truly everywhere, and your position with respect to salt defined your place in society. At medieval tables, there was only one salt cellar: if you sat "above the salt" you were in the privileged position of eating seasoned food. Being below the salt meant you literally had to eat less well.

Governments too used salt to keep the citizenry in place. The ancient Chinese character for salt is a pictograph that represents tools, brine and an imperial official, so that the very word "salt" is defined by official control of its manufacture.

Because salt is both essential to life and relatively easy to transport, it became a perfect commodity for taxation. Tax revenue from salt helped the Chinese to build the Great Wall. The tax on salt, along with tobacco and alcohol, was the cause of dissatisfaction with Stuart monarchy that led, in part, to the English Civil War.

The two most infamous salt taxes, the French *gabelle* and the Indian salt tax imposed by the British, both led to revolution. The gabelle, a tax on salt that had been in place in France since the middle of the thirteenth century, was long hated by the peasants. With good cause: by the late eighteenth century more than 3,000 people were sentenced each year for crimes against the tax. There were of course many other grievances which led to the revolution, but the salt tax became a powerful symbol of the many abuses a government may heap upon its people.

The other revolution was more peaceful: on March 12, 1930, Mahatma Gandhi embarked on a march from Gujarat to Dandi on the Arabian Sea coast of India, in protest against the oppressive salt tax imposed on India by the British. The march left with Gandhi and 78 followers. By the time they had travelled the 385 km (240 m) to the sea, the marchers numbered in their thousands. On April 6, they arrived at Dandi: Gandhi waded into the sea. He walked up the beach until he found a chunk of salt crust that had been evaporated by the sun. He picked it up, proclaiming that with this handful of salt he was proclaiming the end of the British Empire.

The Empire remained, as did the salt tax. But massive subsequent protests ensued, and over time the result was inevitable. Salt would be available to all the people, at a fair price.

Oppression and freedom, good and evil, life and death: we rarely think about these when we sprinkle salt on our chips or throw a spoonful into a pot of boiling water. But perhaps occasionally we should. Because salt, in its own silent way, has a lot of wisdom to impart.

overleaf Lake MacDonnell, near Pengong, western South Australia, produces large amounts of salt.

resources

Salts

HIMALAYAN PINK SALT

Himalayan pink salt is mined from foothills of the Himalayan mountains in Pakistan, where it was deposited when the sea covered the area more than 250 million years ago. Himalayan pink salt is still extracted from mines by hand, according to long-standing tradition, and without the use of any mechanical devices or explosion techniques. Often the salt is brought down from the mountains on the backs of yaks. After being hand-selected, the salt is then hand-crushed, hand-washed and dried in the sun. The unrefined pink transluscent crystals have a subtle, crunchy texture. Try with barbecued meats, vegetables or highly spiced food. The gentle flavour of this salt will not compete with the spices.

HIMALAYAN SALT BLOCK

Cut from slabs of solid crystal salt, the Himalayan salt block may be chilled to freezing point or heated to over 230°C (445°F), making it ideal for serving a range of hot or cold foods. The blocks are carved from slabs of pure salt that is estimated to be up to 250 million years old. They look a little like pink marble, but one touch with the tongue confirms that they are indeed made of salt. Available in a range of sizes, the Himalayan salt block is an innovative way to cook, cure and serve food.

FLEUR DE SEL DE GUÉRANDE

Fleur de sel, the "flower of the salt", is the name used for salt that has been raked by hand from salt ponds surrounding certain villages in France. It is harvested from May to September by artisan paludiers, who patiently wait as the shallow pools of water in the salt ponds evaporate, creating the prized salt crystals, which may only be collected when the weather is warm and winds are light. Each day a new layer of salt rises to the top of the pond, crystallising in delicate flakes.

Fleur de sel de Guérande has long been prized by chefs and gourmets for its high quality. Light and flaky with a pure, slightly mineral taste, it is perfect for finishing dishes, either in the kitchen or at the table. Add to fresh garden vegetables and delicate sauces, and use for flavouring seafood such as oysters, prawns (shrimp) and scallops.

KEY TO SALTS

1. Himalayan pink salt, coarse
2. Himalayan pink salt, fine
3. Netherlands smoked salt
4. Fleur de sel de Camargue
5. Hawaiian black salt
6. Kala namak (Indian black salt)
7. Sicilian sea salt
8. Fleur de sel de Guérande
9. Hawaiian green salt
10. Hawaiian 'Alaea red salt
11. Murray River pink salt
12. Tetsuya's truffle salt
13. Olsson's macrobiotic sea salt
14. Halon Môn sea salt
15. Maldon sea salt
16. Cyprus black salt
17. Cyprus lemon salt

OLSSON'S SEA SALT

Olsson's sea salt is made in Australia in Queensland and South Australia using solar evaporation; the seawater evaporates in successive ponds until it is fully concentrated with crystallised salt. After the salt crystallises it is gathered and washed in seawater; the salt is then dried in a kiln and packaged.

Olsson's sea salt has a bright, pure, clean flavour, which many consider carries the tang of the ocean. It is an ideal general-purpose salt, suitable for both seasoning and finishing at the table, and is a good choice for flavouring fish dishes.

MURRAY RIVER PINK SALT

Drawn from brine springs that would otherwise contaminate the Murray-Darling Basin in Victoria, Australia, Murray River salt has quickly gained a reputation around the world as an excellent finishing salt, subtle in flavour and rich in minerals. The salmon-pink colour is unique to the location and contains minerals—such as magnesium, potassium, iron and calcium—not commonly found in other salt waters. The red pigment, carotene, is secreted from salt-tolerant algae and found in varying strength throughout the Murray River basin. Flake sizes vary with seasonal conditions as warmer weather speeds evaporation, whereas milder weather allows the crystals more time to develop, making them larger as a result. The soft colour is matched by a light, delicate texture that crumbles easily in the fingers. Great with a good steak or other grilled, roasted or barbecued meats; the soft, earthy flavour goes well with vegetables such as mushrooms and potatoes.

HALEN MÔN SEA SALT

The pure white, crunchy flakes of Halen Môn are produced in a way that marries centuries-old craft with high technology. The salt-making process begins with pure charcoal-filtered seawater drawn from Wales' Menai Straits. The water is first naturally filtered through a mussel bed and then a sandbank, which ensures the water is completely pure. The filtered water is gently heated in a vacuum that encourages it to almost boil at a low temperature. As the water releases steam it is concentrated into very salty brine. The steam that is produced is used, in its turn, to heat the brine. When the concentration of salt in the water is high enough it is released into shallow crystallisation tanks.

Overnight delicate crystals begin to form, first on the surface then sinking as they grow. In the morning the salt is harvested by gently scooping out the flakes. This process means that Halen Môn is a very good salt to use when less delicacy of taste and texture is required. Use it to accompany seafood, white meat such as pork or chicken, and on fresh fruit such as melon. Excellent with chocolate and other sweets.

MALDON SALT

Maldon salt, with its delicate, pyramid-shaped crystals, has been produced from the Atlantic waters near the Maldon region of Essex, England, since the Middle Ages. It has become one of the most popular of all sea salts, used in restaurant kitchens around the world.

A beautifully mild, flaky salt, from the Atlantic rather than the Mediterranean, Maldon salt is recommended as much for its texture as its flavour: the large crystals are easy to pick up with the fingers and can then be crumbled to the desired consistency. The flavour is mild, without bitterness or metallic aftertaste. This makes it ideal for foods with subtle flavours, and for adding to sweets, particularly chocolate. It pairs well with delicate, sweet fish and is especially suitable for fresh vegetables and salads.

CYPRUS BLACK SEA SALT

This salt is unlike any other salt in the world—its sensational black colour makes it stand out, but it is also quick to dissolve, both on the tongue and on hot foods. The salt is initially white, and then activated with charcoal from volcanic areas. The colour makes it a dramatic garnishing salt, adding an exciting visual appeal. It pairs extraordinarily well with tomatoes and mushrooms.

CYPRUS LEMON SALT FLAKES

These sea salt flakes from the Mediterranean that have been enhanced by lemon enable dishes to be seasoned with two essential flavourings at once. Particularly useful for rich or sweet dishes that benefit being "cut" with the tang of citrus, or as an alternative to soy sauce for sushi and sashimi.

TETSUYA'S TRUFFLE SALT

The black truffle is one of the most sought-after foods in the world; it is also one of the most expensive. An ideal way to add the taste of black truffle to food is to add it to salt, which is an ideal medium for carrying both the strong aroma as well as the delicate flavour of the truffle.

Tetsuya's truffle salt is a delicate and aromatic blend of ground black truffle and sea salt, sourced from Italy, which brings the unique aroma of truffle to everyday dishes, turning them into something exotic and exciting. Try with cooked egg dishes, tossed in pasta, on paté or foie gras or sprinkled on buttered popcorn.

SICILIAN SEA SALT

Italian sea salt is produced from the low waters of the Mediterranean Sea along the coast of Sicily. It is a natural salt rich in minerals such as iodine, fluorine, magnesium and potassium with a much lower percentage of sodium chloride than regular table salt. The salt pans are filled with the seawater in the spring and left to evaporate relying on the heat of the Sicilian sun and strong African winds. Harvesting takes place once the water has evaporated and the salt is crushed and ground without further refining. It has a delicate taste and plenty of flavour without being too strong or salty. It is particularly good as a highlight to salads, finishing roast meats and in sauces. Great as a garnish on bruschetta. Its gentleness also goes well with soft, delicate fish.

KALA NAMAK (INDIAN BLACK SALT)

Also known as black salt or sanchal, kala namak is an unrefined volcanic table salt with a strong sulphuric flavour. Despite its name, this salt, which is mined in Central India, is actually light pink in color. It is rich in minerals and most often used to flavour Indian dishes such as chaats, vegetable and fruit salads.

The unique taste of Indian black salt can be enjoyed on many different foods and dishes, and not necessarily confined to Indian cuisine. Fruit, particularly citrus fruit, is greatly enhanced. Great with yoghurt and cheese or sprinkled on cucumbers, watermelon and mangoes, and in lemonade.

NETHERLANDS SMOKED SALT

The effects of smoke on salt are quite remarkable: the smoke clings to the surface of the salt crystals, coating them with a rich, woody colour and imparting a strong, smoky flavour. And when the salt dissolves, that flavour goes straight into the food.

People have been smoking their salt since at least the time of the Vikings, who produced salt by evaporating seawater in a big vessel over an open, smoky fire containing juniper, cherry, elm beech and oak woods. In modern times, the salt is often produced first, then subsequently smoked.

This fine smoked salt from the Netherlands will bring out the umami (savoury) flavour in every dish. It is perfect as an addition to sauces and marinades. Try with barbecued meats, barbecued vegetables and seafood to accentuate the smokiness.

HALEN MÔN VANILLA

Salt is the ideal medium for carrying other flavours. The unique pyramid-shaped crystal of sea salt is here enhanced with vanilla. This is a surprisingly versatile salt, which will bring life to a range of different foods. It goes well with savoury flavours and gives a unique twist to seafood, especially to sweet fish and scallops, and is also good on fruit.

HAWAIIAN 'ALAEA RED SALT

These salts take their name from the iron-oxide-rich red volcanic clay, called 'Alaea, which gives them colour. Harvested on the Hawaiian island of Kauai, which is their only source, these are claimed to have the highest concentration of trace minerals and elements of all salt. Authentic 'Alaea red clay will cause a fizzing reaction when added to a liquid, and imparts a subtle, mellow flavour to the salt. Its earthy mineral taste goes well with any red meat or vegetables.

HAWAIIAN GREEN SALT

Green bamboo-leaf extract blended with pure sea salts from the Pacific Ocean produce this delicate flavoured salt. Like other dramatically coloured salts, this green salt is an ideal for garnishing plates, or served separately at the table. Try it with Asian foods as well as white fish, salads and steamed or grilled vegetables.

Measurements and Conversions

DRY MEASURE

Metric	oz (US)
8 g	¼ oz
15 g	½ oz
30 g	1 oz
60 g	2 oz
90 g	3⅛ oz
120 g	4¼ oz
140 g	5 oz
175 g	6⅛ oz
200 g	7oz
225 g	8 oz
285 g	10 oz
450 g	16 oz (1 lb)
675 g	1½ lb
900 g	2 lb
1 kg	2¼ lb
1.5 kg	3¼ lb
2 kg	4½ lb
2.3 kg	5 lb

Note:

The measurements in this book list the metric measurement followed by the equivalent US measurement in parentheses.

LIQUID MEASURE

Metric	Imperial	fl oz (US)
5 ml	1 tsp	
15 ml	1 tbsp	½ fl oz
30 ml	2 tbsp	1 fl oz
60 ml	3 tbsp	2 fl oz
75 ml	4 tbsp	2½ fl oz
100 ml		3½ fl oz
150 ml		5 fl oz
300 ml		10 fl oz
475 ml		16 fl oz (1 pint)
600 ml		1¼ pint
750 ml		1½ pint
900 ml		2 pint
1 l		2⅛ pint

OVEN TEMPERATURES

Description	°C	°F	gas mark
very cool	110	230	¼
cool	130	265	½
warm	160	320	3
	180	355	4
medium	190	375	5
fairly hot	200	390	6
	220	430	7
hot	230	445	8
very hot	250	480	9

Index of Recipes

almonds, Spanish	76
anchovy paste	120
anchovy-spiced meatballs	103
aniseed salt	46
aromatic salt	48
bananas flambé	128
beans, chilli-salted snake	110
beef, cured Wagyu	62
beef, hot-cured	96
beef, steak	94
biltong	63
black bean sauce	115
bread with chocolate and salt	124
bread, white	79
brine	57–58
brine, flavoured	58
brined feta	143
brined trout	82
broccoli soup	56
butter	140
caper mayonnaise	121
caponata	109
caramel and dark chocolate truffles	127
caramel, salted	126
caramel, salted-butter ice cream	139
caramel, soft vanilla-salted	126
carpaccio, scallop	90
carpaccio, tuna	89
caviar	75
cayenne salt	45
cheese, aged	144
cheese, brined feta	143
cheese, fromage blanc	142
cheese, parmesan	75
cheese, simple	141

cherry tomatoes, slow-roasted	108
chicken, in salt crust	98
chicken, roasted (perfect poultry)	99
Chinese greens	111
chocolate mousse with olive oil and salt	125
chocolate, and caramel truffles	127
chocolate, with bread and salt	124
citrus salt, spicy	48
cocktail, margarita	74
coconut salt	49
confit of duck	100
cooking water, salted	53
crackers, salt	76
crackling, pork	101
cream, pastry	136
dashi	55
dill pickles	69
dressing, miso	117
dressing, umeboshi and parsley	118
duck confit	100
dulce de leche	137
feta, brined	143
fish, fillets baked in salt	84
fish, whole baked in salt	83
flambé, bananas	128
focaccia, olive and rosemary	78
French fries	106
fromage blanc	142
fruit, roasted in salt	129
garlic salt oil	59
garlic sausages	67
gomashio	46
gravlax	66
gravy, salt pork	121

Index of Recipes (*contd*)

green papaya salad	111	oil, with garlic and salt	59
green sauce	119	olive and rosemary focaccia	78
greens, in oyster sauce	111	olives	69
greens, salad	110		
		pan con chocolate y sal	124
ham, sweet-cured	65	papaya, green	111
herbes salées	68	parmesan	75
homemade salt	43	Parmigiano-Reggiano	75
		parsley dressing, with umeboshi	118
ice cream, salted-butter caramel	139	pastry cream	136
ice cream, vanilla with Murray River pink salt	138	pastry, sweet short-crust	130
Indian marinade, spicy	48	pickles, dill	69
		pickles, kimchi	71
kimchi	71	porcini salt	49
		pork, roasted	101
lamb, salt-baked	97	pork, salt	64
lavender salt	47	pork, crackling	101
lemon, salted		potatoes and garlic	107
lemons, preserved	68	potatoes, French-fried	106
		prawns (shrimp), barbecued with Bay salt	86
macarons, salted caramel	132	prawns (shrimp), cooked in rock salt	85
margarita	74	preserved lemons	68
marinade, spicy Indian	48	pretzels, soft	77
mayonnaise, caper	121	prik-kab-klua	49
meatballs, anchovy-spiced	103	prosciutto, with melon balls	74
melon and prosciutto	74		
Merguez sausages	102	roast chicken	99
meringues	131	roast pork	101
miso dressing	117	rosemary salt	47
mousse, chocolate with olive oil and salt	125		
Murray River pink salt, vanilla ice cream	138	salad, simple	110
		salad, green papaya	111
nuoc cham, Thai dipping sauce	114	salmon, gravlax	66
nuts, salted	76	salmon, on salt block	88
		salt and pepper squid	87
oil, salty	59	salt baking, chicken	98
oil, smoked chilli salt	59	salt baking, fish fillets	84

salt baking, fruit 129
salt baking, lamb 97
salt baking, whole fish 83
salt-block salmon 88
salt crackers 76
salt pork 64
salt pork gravy 121
salt-roasted fruit 129
salt, aniseed 46
salt, aromatic 48
salt, coconut 49
salt, lavender 47
salt, porcini 49
salt, rosemary 47
salt, Sichuan 46
salt, tarragon 47
salt, vanilla 49
salt, with bread and chocolate 124
salted almonds 76
salted caramel 126
salted butter caramel ice cream 139
salted caramel macarons 132
salted water 53
salting, steak 94
salty oil 59
sauce, black bean 115
sauce, green 119
sauce, soy 116
sauerkraut 70
sausages, garlic 67
sausages, Merguez 102
sea salt 42
scallop carpaccio 90
scallops with vanilla salt 90
short-crust pastry, sweet 130
Sichuan salt 46
smoked chilli salt 44

smoked chilli salt oil 59
snake beans, chilli-salted 110
soffrito, basic 52
soft caramel, vanilla-salted 126
soup, broccoli 56
soy sauce 116
Spanish almonds 76
squid, salt and pepper 87
steak, salted 94
stock 54
sweet short-crust pastry 130
sweet-cured ham 65

tapenade 120
tarragon salt 47
Thai dipping sauce, nuoc cham 114
tomatoes, salt-roasted vine 108
tomatoes, slow-roasted cherry 108
trout, brined 82
truffles, caramel and dark chocolate 127
tuna carpaccio 89

umeboshi and parsley dressing 118

vanilla ice cream with Murray River pink salt 138
vanilla salt 49
vanilla-salted soft caramel 126
vine tomatoes, salt-roasted 108

Wagyu beef, cured 62
water, salted 53
white bread 79

Bibliography

Beard, Trevor. *Salt Matters: A Consumer Guide*, Lothian, 2004
Cook, Slavin and Jones. *Salt & Pepper, the Cookbook*, Chronicle Books, 2003
David, Elizabeth. *Spices, Salt and Aromatics in the English Kitchen*, Grub Street, 2000
Hay, Donna. *Off The Shelf*, HarperCollins, 2001
Jordan, Michele Anna. *Salt and Pepper*, Broadway Books, 1999
Kurlansky, Mark. *Salt: A World History*, Vintage, 2003
Larousse Gastronomique, Clarkson Potter, 2001
McGee, Harold. *McGee on Food and Cooking*, Hodder and Stoughton, 2004
McGee, Harold. *On Food and Cooking*, Scribner, 2004
McLagen, Jennifer. *Fat*, Ten Speed Press, 2008
Ruhlman, Michael. *Charcuterie: The Craft of Salting, Smoking, and Curing*, W. W. Norton & Company, 2005
Ruhlman, Michael. *The Elements of Cooking*, Black Inc., 2007
Sandler, Nick and Acton, Johnny. *Preserved*, Kyle Cathie, 2004
Tarantino, Jim. *Marinades, Rubs, Brines, Cures & Glazes*, Ten Speed Press, 2006
This, Hervé, *Molecular Gastronomy*, Columbia University Press, 2006
Steingarten, Jeffrey. *The Man Who Ate Everything*, Headline, 1997
Vassallo, Jody. *Salt and Pepper*, Hachette Livre, 2005
von Bremzen, Anya. *The New Spanish Table*, Workman Publishing, 2006

Credits

Photographs: Scott Cameron pp 2, 12–13, 15, 20, 23, 25–29, 34, 36, 37, 39, 40, 51, 61, 73, 81, 91, 93, 95, 105, 113, 122, 133, 135 and cover; F1online pp 146–147, 152–153; Stock Connection pp 158–159; Corbis pp 164–165; Getty Images pp 170–171; Alimdi pp 176–177; Photononstop pp 182–183; Age Fotostock pp 188–189; The Art Archive/Global Book Publishing pp 194–195.

PROPS FOR PHOTOGRAPHY

Alfresco Emporium: black salt bowl pp 36–37; cocktail glasses and cocktail shaker pp 73.
Clay & Flax: linen place mat p 34; chocolate napkin p 61.
Dinosaur Designs: egg scoop dish pp 12–13; Calder soy dish pp 17, 123, 203; shell side plate p 26; spoons pp 28, 29, 135; shell gelato cup pp 39, 93; Calder side plates and shell soy dish p 51; egg bowl p 105; Calder stabile plate p 135.
Macarons on pp 119 and 129, Adriano Zumbo, Zumbo Patisserie.

Acknowledgements

We would like to thank James Ballingal, Program Director for Culinary Arts, and the team at William Blue College of Hospitality Management, for their assistance. We would also like to thank everyone who has participated in one of our salt tasting events and offered their observations and opinions about salt.

My Tasting Notes

My Tasting Notes